Every book is a symbol...

Editor-in-Chief
Nihat YALÇIN

Author
Dr. Raşit GÜNDOĞDU

Editor
Harun TUNCER

Grafics&Design
iletisim.media

Translation
A-Tercüme

Original Title
Bir Siyasî Dehanın Portresi:
Sultan Abdülhamid

RUMUZ
PUBLISHING

1. Edition: İstanbul, Nisan 2019
Limit Ofset Metin ESKİBAĞ
Address: Maltepe Mah. Litros Yolu 2.
Matbaacılar Sitesi No:2-4 D: ZA-13
Zeytinburnu/İSTANBUL
Phone: 0212 567 45 35
Certificate Number: 28397

ISBN: 978-605-5112-86-8

Address: Muratreis Mah. Nuhkuyusu
Cad. No: 295/2 Üsküdar / İSTANBUL
Phone: 0216 530 07 50
www.rumuzyayinlari.com
rumuzyayinlari@gmail.com

T.C. Kültür Bakanlığı Yayıncılık
Certificate Number: 27601

The Portrait of a Political Genius:
Sultan Abdulhamid II

Rumuz Publishing: 72
History Series: 24

The Portrait of a Political Genius

Sultan Abdulhamid II

Rumuz
PUBLISHING

Contents

FOREWORD

Sultan Abdulhamid was one of the most important and controversial figures of the 19th century. Due to both the important occurrences of this "long century" and the many years of reign enjoyed by the Sultan helped him play a decisive role in the Turkish history.

Sultan was ruling a land still known as the most proper part of the globe to be exploited in an era when imperialism was harshly colonizing the "under-developed" world. And just because of that he was a man that was hardly liked. As being one of the formidable leaders of the times when the classical conflict between the East and the West was evolving toward a very bloody fight, Sultan Abdulhamid was thought to be born for defense. Even deeply immersed in an intensive conflict both inside and outside the country, the Sultan was striving for the wellbeing of his people and his domain.

In this study the writer tried to shed some light upon the personal life of the Sultan and to panoramically narrate his work as a statesman. He was also concerned for the language and style to be clear and objective; and for being able to present the reader a more imaginable text he enriched the work with visuals.

INTRODUCTION AND PHOTOGRAPH

Father: Abdulmejid Han

Mother: Tîr-i Müjgân Sultan

Birth: 21 September 1842

Succession to the throne: 31 August 1876

Spouses: Nâzikedâ, Bedrifelek Nûrefsun, Bîdâr, Dilpesend, Mezide, Emsâlinur, Müşfika

Offspring: Mehmed Selim, Abdulkâdir, Ahmed Nuri, Burhaneddin, Abdurrahim, Nureddin, Bedreddin, Mehmed Âbid and Ulviye Zekiye, Nâime Nâile, Şadiye, Refia, Ayşe sultans

Dethronement: 1909

Death: 10 February 1918

Tomb: Mahmud II Tomb, Çemberlitaş, Istanbul

Order: 99th Islamic Caliph, 34th Ottoman Sultan

Sultan Abdulmajid, Hamid's father

On 31 August 1876 (10 Shaban 1293) Thursday, Sultan Murad V was removed from the Ottoman throne which he had reigned for 93 days. He was replaced with Abdulhamid Han as the 34th Ottoman Sultan.

On 7 September, the new sultan girded a sword in Eyup Sultan Mosque. He visited the tombs of ancestors with a large ceremonial entourage. Hundreds of thousands of people were cheering along the roads and on the shore to greet the sultan as the entourage progressed from Edirnekapı to Topkapı Palace.

In the meantime, the naval vessels were greeting the new sultan with artillery fire, the enthronement was celebrated with cannon fire from different parts of Istanbul.

Sultan Abdulhamid, sat himself in the golden throne established in front of the Babüssaade, while all the state dignitaries pledged their allegiance one by one. The Sultan accepted the grand vizier, sheik al-Islam and the high state dignitaries in the audience hall.

When Abdulhamid heard that his brother Murad V had been transferred to Ciragan Palace he boarded the imperial caique and left for Dolmabahce Palace.

This was how he spent the first day of his reign that would last 33 years.

Dolmabahçe Palace, Constantinople

PRINCEDOM

A CAUTIOUS AND INTELLIGENT PRINCE

Prince Abdulhamid who was born as the son of Sultan Abdulmejid and Tirimüjgân KadınEffendi was two years younger than his brother Murad V. At the age of 11, his mother passed away (31 October 1852). Abdulhamid was delivered to the loving care of Perestû Kadın Effendi, a wife of Sultan Mecid who had no children of her own. When he was 18 he lost his father Albülmecid Han and his uncle Abdulaziz Han ascended to the throne and since his children were small, the two children of Abdulmejid Han became crown princes.

Prince Abdulhamid and his brother Murad Effendi received a good education together. They were instructed by renown names in their fields such as Edhem Pasha, Kemal Pasha, Saffet Pasha, Gardet, Gerdankıran Ömer Effendi, Ferid Effendi, Şerif Effendi, Ali Mahvî Effendi, Vak'anüvis (Chronicler) Lütfi Effendi, Guatelli, Lombardi. They received instruction in Turkish, Arabic, Farsi, French. They learned how to use weapons, riding and similar military skills first from the teachers and then from military officers.

He was instructed in interpretation, hadith and Islamic law by Gümüşhânevî Ömer Hulûsî Effendi. He learned about Ottoman history from Vak'anüvis Lütfi Effendi. The Sultan was extremely interested in history. His respect for science and scientist was enormous. Abdulhamid Han had been following the local and foreign press since his princedom and would continue to follow the foreign press closely throughout his reign.

Abdulhamid Han, a good calligrapher and carpenter, has been involved in trade since his princedom. He had a carpenter's workshop and farms, and had a wealth of experience operating a mine. In the future, he would use his private assets generously in the service of the state when necessary.

Furniture allegedly used by Sultan Hamid

The wooden products made by the Sultan were arty enough to gain the admiration of master carpenters. Some of his works are still used in Yıldız Palace and Mosque. Prince Abdulhamid was distinguished by his intelligence and extremely strong memory. His political ability, moderate and frugal behavior attracted the attention of his uncle, Sultan Abdulaziz. As a matter of fact, Sultan Abdulaziz Han mobilized all means for his upbringing. Sultan Abdulaziz's taking Abdulhamid Han with him on his travels to Egypt and Europe would make a significant contribution in the raising of the most powerful last sultan of the Ottoman Empire.

TRAVELS TO EGYPT AND EUROPE

In 1863, Sultan Aziz decided to travel suddenly to Egypt. For the first time ever since the conquest of Sultan Yavuz Selim an Ottoman Sultan was going to Egypt. Abdulaziz Han had strengthened the reform and systematizing struggles of his father, Mahmud II and aimed to establish a state dominance in a broad sense. Khidiv Ismail, one of the offspring of Kavalali Mehmed Ali Pasha, who rebelled during his father's reign in Egypt, was in charge of administration.

Mehmed Ali Pasha, governor of Egypt and the man who had a fatal role in the destruction of the Empire (L'Illustration Journal Universal)

Abdulaziz Han was accompanied by Abdulhamid and his brother, Murad V on his trip to Egypt. They traveled from Istanbul to Alexandria by sea and then to Cairo by train. Prince Abdulhamid, who was 21 years old then, experienced traveling by train, which was not popular in the Ottoman Empire at that time but was built by the Kavalali family between Alexandria and Cairo. Egyptian people welcomed the sultan with great enthusiasm.

After his trip to Egypt, Sultan Abdulaziz went on a tour of Europe with a distinguished delegation. He took the first heir apparent to the throne, prince Murad and the second heir apparent Abdulhamid with him as he had done to Egypt.

Sultan Abdulaziz (Encyclopedia Britannica)

On June 21, 1967, two ships and two accompanying Ottoman destroyers and one patrol ship set off. The Sultan was accompanied by the Minister of Foreign Affairs and about forty statesmen.

Sultan Abdulaziz went to France by sea and traveled to Paris via Tulon-Marseille for ten days and visited the important venues of Paris. The Sultan was honoring the invitation of the French Emperor Napoleon III to the Universal Exhibition in France. He met the Emperor of France Napoleon III and Empress Eugenie. In the meantime, they witnessed the welcome demonstrations of the Parisians. Thus the sultan saw modern Europe and dreamed of innovations in the Ottoman country.

The Sultan and his entourage crossed over the English Channel to Dover and from there to London. Here they met Queen Victoria. After 11 days in the British capital they travelled to the Black Sea coast over Belgium, Germany-Austria-Hungary. They returned to Istanbul by taking the Sultaniye yacht that had taken the sultan to France. The trip lasted 47 days. This tour which included diplomatic visits was the first in Ottoman history. For the first time, an Ottoman sultan officially visited foreign countries. During these visits, Abdulaziz Han and his delegation went to eight countries and met five rulers. (Emperor of France, Napoleon III, Queen Victoria of England, King Leopold II of Belgium, King Wilhelm I of Prussia, Emperor of Austria and King of Hungary Francis Joseph, Prince of Romania Karol I).

Napoleon III, the French Emperor

Abdulhamid Han saw many presidents, diplomats, administrative places, palaces, pavilions on his trips to Egypt and Europe, he attended fairs, meetings, museums, he had the opportunity to explore the military order of different countries, weapons technologies and technical developments. Thus, he got ideas for future developments and projects, widened his horizon.

HOW DID THE PATH TO THE SULTANATE OPEN?

The 32nd Ottoman Sultan, Abdulaziz Han was deposed by a coup in 1876 and martyred and his nephew Prince Murad succeeded to the throne. Ambitious statesmen who had been cajoled by foreign states had become so effective in the state order that they could now jeopardize the life of the sultan and take the throne of a new sultan.

However, as the course of divinity would have it, contrary to the plans of those who want to seize the administration of the state, Sultan Murad was deeply affected by his uncle's murder and lost his mental faculties. In fact, it was thought that he would behave in an unbalanced manner among the people and he had not even been exposed to the sword dressing ceremony which had been the spiritual submittal tradition of the caliphate for centuries. Sultan Murad became ill one week after his accession. Murad V's spiritual tremors were gradually increasing. When he began to display errant behavior in a short time, it was impossible for him to remain on the throne. When the treatment of the doctors gave no results, it was decided that the other crown prince, Prince Abdulhamid would succeed.

However, there was a second view of the Ottoman administration among the statesmen. Grand Vizier Midhat Pasha and some of his supporters wanted Murad V to be on the throne, and Abdulhamid Han to be a head of state serving as a prince regent. This was because Sultan Abdulaziz had been deposed by a coup. The termination of a second sultan in such a short time could have led to bad repercussions. Furthermore, the team that had ended the reign of Sultan Aziz was more likely to be able to dominate the rule of a prince regent without full power.

Prince Abdulhamid did not accept this offer. He wanted the presidency to be represented by a real sultan. He met with Sadrazam Rüşdü Pasha and Midhat Pasha and made some promises to them. He reportedly supported the declaration of the constitutional monarchy. On this, Murad V was deposed and his brother Abdulhamid II replaced him on the throne.

Former governor and vizier Midhat Pasha

TRANSITION TO THE SULTANATE

THE FIRST MONTHS

The draft copy of the imperial order that Sultan Abdulhamid would publish at his accession was prepared by Midhat Pasha. The new sultan made some changes in the pasha's text and had it published as he wished. He ordered the convening of a National Assembly and a parliament composed of ministers, ulema and jurists for the preparation of constitutional laws in accordance with the traditions and customs as well as Sharia provisions.

Said Pasha, the Younger

Ahmed Mukhtar Pasha

Within a few days of taking over the throne, the Sultan met with all the deputies and received detailed information about the status of the country.

Initially he started by cutting down on the palace expenses. He appointed the Finance Minister Galib Pasha to examine all the palace expenses and started to implement savings measures. On the other hand, from time to time he received instruction from Jorj Zarifi, one of the famous bankers of Istanbul, in order to increase his financial knowledge.

During the first months of his reign he often went outside the palace. He had dinner with land and naval officers, and he visited hospitals. He prayed with the people in mosques, met with scholars. He made ferry trips in Marmara and the Straits and gave feasts in the palace. This version of the Sultan gave a very positive impression in his vicinity, it made him more popular.

The sultan had some preformed ideas about state administration. He believed in appointing honest and competent people to work. One of his first actions was to appoint Mahmud Jalaluddin Pasha as Chamberlain. The great Said Pasha who had been educated in the United Kingdom and nicknamed "English" was appointed to the Ministry for Defense.

Since the appointing of the Chamberlain and Minister for Defense was within the authority of the Sultan the deputies did not object. However, when it was time to appoint the chief clerk and clerks, their tune changed. Vizier Rüşdü Pasha and Midhat Pasha wanted Sadullah Bey to be appointed as chief clerk, the person closest and most influential with the sultan and Namık Kemal and Ziya Bey to be appointed clerks. Contrary to what had been said earlier, Sultan Abdulhamîd Han appointed Küçük Said Pasha, member of the Trade and Agriculture Assembly as chief clerk of the chamberlain and Lebib Bey, Chief of Criminal Appeals Court as chamberlain clerk.

On these decisions of Sultan Abdulhamid Han, who wanted to retain control of the state in the first days of his reign, Grand Vizier Rüşdü Pasha wanted to resign but his resignation was not accepted by the sultan.

Hussein Avni Pasha

The rebellion of the Serbs and Montenegro, which had begun before the sultan's accession, was continuing. The Ottoman operation under the command of Abdulkerim Nâdir and Ahmed Mukhtar pashas against the Serbs and Montenegrins, who had been instigated to rebel with the support and provocation of the Russians continued. In Crete, restlessness was at its peak. Russia was preparing for war to grab the biggest share of the state in this confusion.

With the positive atmosphere of the approach of the new Ottoman sultan in terms of the army and statesmen, the army started to gain significant successes on the Serbian front. When the Ottoman army was about to enter Belgrade, the big states intervened. On November 1, 1876, a two-month ceasefire was signed with Serbia at the request of Russia to immediately end the war.

Abdulhamid Han was aware of the economic and political crises in which the state was. Although his uncle Abdulaziz had made many innovations with his forward-thinking activities, sedition and intrigue had spread to the administrative staff within the palace.

He had not forgotten about the coup that Midhat Pasha, Serasker Hussein Avni Pasha, Mütercim Mehmed Rüşdü Pasha and Sheikh al-Islam Hasan Hayrullah Effendi had carried out against his uncle with sixty military personnel they had engaged. On 30 May 1876, they besieged Dolmabahce Palace and deposed the sultan. After Sultan Abdulaziz Han left Dolmabahce Palace, a large part of his belongings and money were looted by some opportunistic coup plotters. The personal wealth of Sultan Abdulaziz Han was confiscated and a decision was taken by the commission for the transfer of his money to the treasury. The jewelry was sent to Paris to be sold there on the grounds that they would get a better price but it never came back, nor were they compensated.

Abdulaziz Han asked his nephew Murad V to be transferred to Fer'iye Palace, which was located next to Çırağan Palace in Ortaköy and is used as a restaurant today (June 1, 1876). The former sultan was taken into custody here and martyred under the guise of suicide by three wrestlers pretending to be servants.

This incident was sufficient reason for Sultan Hamid to replace seafront Dolmabahce and Topkapı Palace with a safe administrative center. Thus, he decided to position Yıldız Palace which had been used by sultans and princes for centuries and belonged to the Treasury as the center of state administration. The construction of the buildings in the Yıldız Palace complex which is still standing was started. In the construction of the palace buildings, the sultan would employ four different architects in order to be the only one in control of all tls.

Feriye Palace where Sultan Abdulaziz was murdered

Belgrade in 1890's

ANNOUNCEMENT OF THE SHIPYARD (TERSANE) CONFERENCE AND CONSTITUTIONAL MONARCHY

As Abdulhamid II was ascending to the throne, the rebellion of the Montenegrin and Serbian princedoms continued. The state was in the middle of a war. Osman Pasha defeated Serbian troops under the command of the Russian general Chernyayev in the battle of Aleksinac and the Ottoman army started to progress towards Belgrade. Being aware of the situation, Russia immediately gave an ultimatum and prevented Belgrade from falling. The ceasefire proposal was accepted by the Ottomans.

Russia did not see any benefits in making Romania or Serbia independent kingdoms. A proposal to organize a conference for the establishment of an autonomous government to protect the interests and right to life of the Christian people living in Bosnia-Herzegovina and Bulgaria and initiate reforms by the Ottoman State was made. Britain was satisfied with this attitude of the tsar. Britain was disturbed by the aggressive intentions of the Russians and their desire to expand towards the south.

Such an intervention by Russia raised alarms in European states. A decision was made to hold a conference in Istanbul to discuss the situation. Subsequently, the Shipyard Conference was held with the participation of foreign state delegates and envoys in Istanbul. According to international law the meeting was to be chaired by the Turkish Minister for Foreign Affairs, Safvet Pasha.

There was feverish work carried out at the Sublime Porte for the conference. Abdulhamid II decided to announce the constitution to obtain a positive result from the conference. A commission consisting of 28 people was established under the leadership of Server Pasha in order to prepare the Constitution. The commission discussed the preliminary draft prepared by Midhat Pasha. A number of items were issued on the insistence of Vizier Rüşdü Pasha, who was opposed to the establishment of the constitutional order and there was a deep disagreement between Mütercim Rüşdü Pasha and Midhat Pasha.

Abdulhamid Han was as yet unable to fully dominate the administration. The ministers were trying to turn him into a state representative sitting in his palace and drag the state into an abyss. In some decisions, the sultan's opinion was not sought. During these works, the new sultan got to know his statesmen better.

Four days before the Shipyard Conference convened, Grand Vizier Mütercim Rüşdü Pasha resigned and on 19 December 1876, Midhat Pasha

Constantinople Conference

was appointed in his place. The reason behind the resignation was the allegations that Rüşdü Pasha was involved in the state and demise of Sultan Abdulaziz Han.

The Istanbul Conference, also called the 'Shipyard Conference' because it convened in an apartment reserved in the Shipyard started on December 23, 1876. During the conference, the sounds of cannon fire came from outside. Safvet Pasha made a statement saying, 'What you hear is the report of cannon fire heralding the Constitution. The Ottoman State has now become a constitutional monarchy. The rights of the Christian subjects equal the rights of the Muslim people. The concessions that the states demanded have occurred spontaneously.'

That night the buildings in the city were bedecked, torch and firebrand processions were organized. A group of people gathered in front of Dolmabahce Palace, Midhat Pasha's pavilion and the embassies and cheered "Long live the nation, long live the Constitution!" on the streets.

Constantinople, at night (Charles W. Bailey)

Charles W. Bailey, Jr.

On the other hand, the Russian public opinion was waving the banner of Turcophobia and Slavism. Therefore, Midhat Pasha and those around him thought that a few concessions made in the Balkans would curb these feelings. According to Midhat Pasha, the charges against us would be remedied by the Constitution and Europe's intervention would be prevented. However, the powers of the sultan would be limited. With these thoughts the Pasha did not break off with Europe and started to work with the states on condition that the Constitution was guaranteed to immobilize Russia.

At the second session of the conference, the discussions were very tense. Safvet and Edhem Pashas defended the charges against the Ottomans and the rights of the state. In the end, the demands of the delegates were rejected on the grounds that interfering in the internal affairs of a state did not comply with the Constitution and promises that the necessary arrangements would be realized in time.

MIDHAT PASHA IS SENT TO EXILE

On 23 December 1876 (6 December 1293) the Constitution and the First Constitutional Monarchy were written and read by Sultan Abdulhamid in the Sublime Porte. Midhat Pasha had prepared the draft constitution together with a delegation. This delegation also included Ziya Pasha and Namik Kemal. Abdulhamid Han changed some of the articles such as the one that put the Constitution under the guarantee of the European states and that every element in the state could formally use its own language. One of the articles that he considered deleting was the one that announced that sultans could order persons into exile. Such a provision was against the principles of Reform. When Sultan Abdulhamid voiced this, Midhat Pasha insisted on the acceptance of the matter. He wanted to

Shale Kiosk, the Room for Royal Procession

use this article against his opponents. Indeed, after the entry into force of the Constitution, Midhat Pasha would exile many of his opponents.

When the new constitution was announced in the accompaniment of cannon fire the Shipyard Conference continued. Midhat Pasha thought that this innovation would be welcomed by foreign delegates and that the Balkans issue would be resolved easily. The delegates attending the conference were not very interested in the new constitution, and even underrated it. This was a major disappointment for Midhat Pasha.

The proposal for reforms to be made in Bosnia Herzegovina and Bulgaria that was made at the conference to the Sublime Porte was not accepted by the extraordinary assembly of 240 people who gathered in the palace. Midhat Pasha's speeches and the students he had provoked demonstrated in favor of the war which resulted in the rejection of the decisions of the Shipyard Conference. Abdulhamid had to verify the parliament's decision. Thus, a Turco-Russian war was approaching step by step. The likelihood of Turkey warring and defeating Russia alone seemed quite poor.

When the decisions of the conference were not accepted, six state ambassadors left Istanbul. Due to Midhat Pasha's behavior Abdulhamid Han refused to comply with his wishes and left his requests unanswered. Midhat Pasha retired to his home. However, he did not resign. He hoped that the reaction of the people when the sultan dismissed him would be a lesson for the palace. He even thought that if he were dismissed by the sultan, the people would bring him back. He even used the expression "Âl-i Midhat" instead of "Âl-i Osman" in a private gathering.

Previously, Midhat Pasha had provided successful services in the governorships of the Danube (Bulgaria) and Baghdad (Iraq) and his fame had crossed the borders. He supported the British, but as a grand vizier, he had not succeeded in state administration. He was acting like a dictator and did not refrain from disrespecting the sultan. He had started to establish an army for himself under the title 'Nation's soldiers'. Those who volunteered for this army stirred unrest in Istanbul and demonstrated in favor of Midhat Pasha in the streets.

Midhat Pasha was invited to the palace on 5 February 1877, but was not given an audience. Chamberlain's general Said Pasha came and collected the seal of the Grand Viziership from him and stated that according to article 113 of the Constitution the sultan had order that he is deported and that the İzzeddin steamer was waiting for him. At his wish, Midhat Pasha was exiled to Italy according to the article that he had insisted be included in the constitution.

On the day that Midhat Pasha was relieved of his duties, the Grand Vizier's seal was handed over to Edhem Pasha, Head of the Council of State.

THE FIRST ASSEMBLY OPENS

The first Ottoman assembly, called the 'assembly of 93' by the people on account of the Julian calendar date that it coincided with, was opened three months after the proclamation of the Constitutional Law. In the meantime the members of parliament were elected.

Resim-16: Opening session of the Constitutional Parliament

On March 19, 1877, the opening ceremony was held in Dolmabahce Palace's grand ceremony hall. A golden throne ornamented with chrysolite was placed into the hall used for ceremonies and allegiance occasions. The ministers, ulema and state dignitaries took their position around this throne according to the order of state protocol. The members of the Assembly stood opposite the throne, the dignitaries on the right and the ministers on the left. Ahmet Wafik Pasha was appointed chairman. Abdulhamid Han sat on the throne accompanied by the heir apparent and prince, Mehmed Reşâd and Kemâleddin, respectively. He handed over his opening speech to the Grand Vizier Edhem Pasha who passed it along to Said Bey, who was chief clerk (and would later become grand vizier and be called "Youn-

ger"). Said Bey read the statement which took half an hour. Subsequently prayers were offered. Cannons were fired in various parts of the city.

In this statement, the status of the state was explained, the sultan's will in terms of the declaration of the constitutional law and opening of parliament was expressed. Subjects of various religion and nationalities were invited to gather and unite around the idea of Ottomanism.

The first assembly consisted of 120 deputies and 26 dignitaries. Of the 120 deputies, 71 were Muslim, 49 were Christian, Armenian and Jewish. The Muslim MPs belonged to different ethnic elements. It was a parliament where the Turks were a minority. The first Assembly of Deputies worked for about a hundred days and the meetings ended on June 28, 1877. In the second period, which started on December 13, 1877, there were 56 Muslim deputies and 40 Christian deputies. However, among the Muslims, there were members of different elements including Arab, Bosnians, Albanian Abaza, Kurds and Circassians. Most of them were people who were in parliament with a non-Muslim and racist mentality. Some of them did not even speak Turkish. Ahmed Wafik Pasha was the chairman of the first parliamentary session, trying to manage this mixed group.

Opening ceremony of the First Ottoman Parliament at the Dolmabahce Palace in 1876

Ahmed Wafik Pasha

Before long, voices started to emerge against the state and the country in Parliament. Members of different religions and races demanded concessions in the name of the masses they represented, proposing that their language is accepted as the official language, in fact some even sought independence.

THE SULTAN'S ASSEMBLY SPEECH

Sultan Abdulhamid's speech on March 19, 1877 in the First Assembly:

Delegation of Dignitaries, Deputies;

I declare my satisfaction with the opening of the General Assembly, which is a first in our state. You all know that the state and nations can only be strong through justice. Even the emergence of our supreme state, propagating its power to the world has been possible with a fair administration and looking out for the rights and interests of people of all classes.

We are all aware of the fact that the late Sultan Mehmed the Conqueror who is one of our great ancestors ensured freedom and the tolerance he displayed in terms of religion and sects. Other supreme ancestors of ours have always complied with this understanding and never prevented the religious and sectarian rituals. It is a consequence of this understanding of justice that the nationalities, languages and denominations of various classes have been able to conserve their characteristics and exist for six hundred years.

Sultan in the early days of his reign

In essence, in the past, the state and nation's level of welfare increased with the provision of justice and the protection of laws. However, due to disregard of Sharia or law, regression and decay occurred over time.

Finally, my grandfather, the late Sultan Mahmud II, deposed the trouble generated by the janissary, which emerged with the stagnation and decline of our state that has been continuing for several centuries. He stopped the defeat and destruction that harmed the state and the nation. He opened a door to bring the civilization that Europe has currently reached to our homeland. My father, the late Abdulmejid Han, went along this path. He declared the principles of Tanzimat-ı Hayriye (Auspicious Re-orderings) which protects the lives, properties, honor and integrity of our people. Since that day, the trade and agriculture of our country and the revenues of the state have increased several times over. Furthermore, laws have been enacted for the regulations we need and the education and learning of sciences have been extended.

These good practices and especially ensuring the security of our state's internal affairs has elevated our state. However, the emergence of the Crimean War prevented further improvement and continued efforts for the country and the people. Until then, while the state treasury did owe no penny to the outside, external loans had to be taken to cover the costs of the war. Thus the door to debt was opened. We have made peace with the contribution of the states that recognize our legitimacy and we thought we had gained time to progress.

However, events turned out to be contrary to all expectations. In other words, through various provocations, the Montenegro and Belgrade and Crete incidents exploded one after another. For this reason, there has been no opportunity to reform and organize the country. Every year we have gathered large armies and we have to keep most of our people under arms. Therefore, our trade and agriculture have come to a full stop. Even when such problems and obstacles have been encountered, spiritual and material enhancement has been achieved. Continuous increase in our revenues for twenty years, the progress of the country and the prosperity of the people are evidence of this. So while disasters followed each other on one hand, an effort has been made by our state to acquire and manufacture weapons of war on land and sea. In the meantime, the inability to keep our income and expenses in a balance led to the increase of our debt and the deterioration of our finance administration. This has created the current extraordinary hardship.

Although the current hardship was caused by the aforementioned events, if the correct way had been found by the finance administration, the distress could have been alleviated and financial balance could have been achieved.

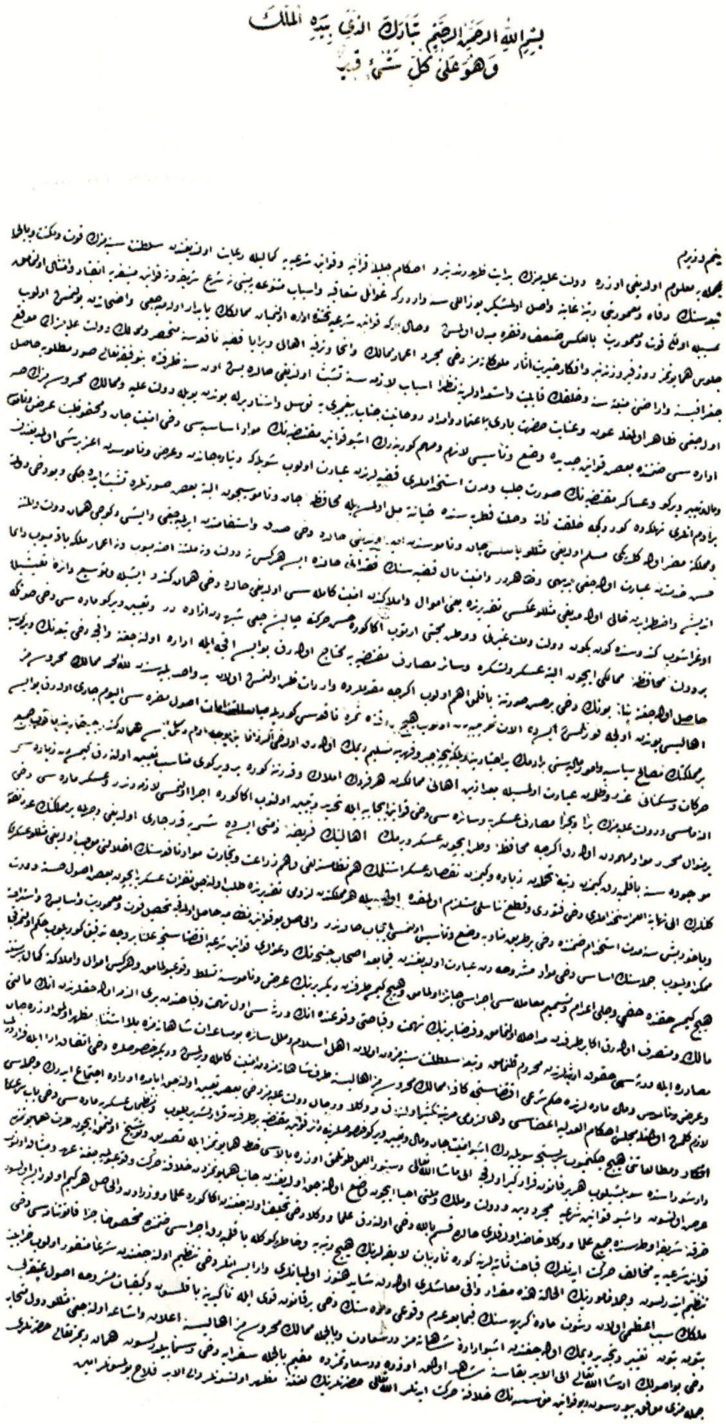
بسم الله الرحمن الرحيم تبارك الذي بيده الملك
وهو على كل شيء قدير

The Edict of Gulhane (1839)

The fiscal measures designed as reform did not improve the situation. In fact, the distress increased further. We have acted without thinking what would happen in the future. Meanwhile, the incidents of Herzegovina grew with some provocations and became very critical. Suddenly war broke out against Serbia and Montenegro. In this turmoil, with the help of the Almighty, in the midst of chaos and political turmoil, I sit upon the throne of my great ancestors.

The problems and dangers were incomparable to any problems previously encountered. In order to protect our legal order I have been obliged to conscript over 600.000 troops. With Allah's help, I see it as my debt to eliminate this confusion completely, make certain fine arrangements and achieve continuous security in our state.

Although it is clear that we can establish a fine administration and reach a very advanced level in a short time we have been unable to reach the present level of development of the civilized world. The reason for this is that the necessary regulations and related laws and statutes have not been maintained and the ones that have been carried out have not been carried out with a constitutional administration.

Whereas the progress of civilized countries, and the safety and development of their countries were enabled by the adoption of general laws that were enacted with the consensus of everyone. Naturally in order to progress, we needed to proceed in this way, the law of the country had to comply with widespread views and have its basis with the people. Therefore, I declared Constitutional Law compliant with Sharia.

Our purpose in enacting the Act is not to invite the public to be ready for all work. This law will be an occasion for the improvement of the administration, the prevention of abuses and the annihilation of the totalitarian regime.

In addition to its main benefits, the Constitutional Law aims to bring unity and brotherhood among races and to establish a happy life and morality for the people. Our great ancestors have conquered many races through successful conquests and collected many races on wide territories under their administration. However, they were unable to bring these nations, which were so different in terms of religion and race under one law and lined to one another with the same feelings. Now, with the help of Allah, who has no end in grace and appreciation, this task will be realized.

Henceforth, all of our people will live under the patronage of the same law as the subjects of the same homeland and continue to live under our patronage of more than six hundred years of glory and honor.

Bosnia during the happy old days or Sarajevo; looking toward Alifakova

I hope that the name 'Ottoman' which has been the symbol of strength and power until now, will ensure the continuation and preservation of prosperity among all our people. That is why I kept moving on this path and I always wanted to stabilize it.

I expect your contributions in order to benefit from the legitimate elements of the Constitutional Law which is based on the rules of law and security.

Now, you must do your legal duties that represent your honor and dignity without any hesitation, without giving a thought to anything else than the honor and happiness of our state and our country in a faithful and guiding manner. Because, the innovations and regulations we need today are very important. And the application of these one by one is possible with the alliance of your ideas and it is in your hands. The laws required by the State Council are also being prepared on the one hand.

In this year's meeting, the internal laws of your parliament, the Law on Elections, the Laws on the Provincial and District Municipalities, the Law on Municipal Offices, the Civil Code and the Law on the Organization of Courts, the Law on the Advancement and the Retirement of Judges, the duties of general officers and the Law on the Right to Retirement, Press (Press) and the Court of Exchequer laws will be referred to your council.

We strongly request you to make your decisions regarding these laws after negotiating and considering them one by one respectively.

In essence, it is imperative that an urgent renewal and regulation is carried out for independent courts which guarantee law for everyone and security-related soldiers. A budget must be allocated for this to be done. However, as you can see from the budget given to your parliament, our financial administration faces many problems and difficulties. Therefore, first of all, we must get rid of this financial trouble and get our financial standing back. On your path in realizing this I would encourage you to take necessary precautions and display diligence.

With the development of agriculture and industry which is needed by our country and our people, increase of civilization and wealth will only be possible by strengthening of science and education. Laws on the renewal of schools and on the organization of learning will be brought to your assembly in the following year Allah permitting.

Appropriate administrative officers must be selected to ensure that the above-mentioned laws and the laws to be introduced subsequently are manifested. Our State will pay attention to this point, as the Constitutional Law has pointed out, that the civil servants are known for their chastity and direction.

I have been aware of the importance of the selection of civil servants since my succession. Therefore, I have designed the establishment of a private school for general administration, which will be covered by our treasury (my own treasury). The students of this school will be employed at the highest level of administration and policy positions. They will be chosen from all classes without exception and be promoted on merit.

In the last period, the internal problems that have been going on for more than two years and the war in Serbia and Montenegro have profoundly saddened us. Nevertheless, the honor shown by all our loyal people and soldiers, the exhibited effort is admirable. In these cases, our experiences with Serbia and Montenegro are the result of our attempts to protect our legal order. The application designed after the negotiations, will be transferred to you in the first session of the Assembly. I recommend that you urgently take your decision on this matter.

Amiable and equal relations with friendly states are among the subjects we care about most. Today we respect these relations.

A few months ago Britain, asked for a conference in Istanbul for issues on the agenda. As other major states have approved the proposed principles, this conference was approved by our Sublime Porte. However, no consensus emerged in this meeting. Nevertheless, we have manifested that our laws are compliant with the provisions of the conventions of the states and the law of nations, and that we have good intentions in terms of the application of wishes and advice.

As to the reasons why there was no compromise, this situation does not arise from the basis of the issue but from the differences in applications. Ever since the beginning of the Reforms to the present, our aim has been to take our country forward and all our work is aimed at this. However, I feel it is my responsibility to protect our country from situations that could undermine its glory and freedom (independence).

I will let time be the witness of the accuracy and soundness of my intentions. It would be more pleasing for me to get rid of the results of this situation as soon as possible. We will always take this path into account in our future actions, as our intent is always to preserve our legal order and independence.

Before and after the gathering of the conference, I hope that our government's measured stance and goodwill will increase the friendship that connects our sovereignty to the Association of European States.

May the Almighty grant us success in our endeavors.

Gateway to the palace and offices of the Grand Vezir (Prime Minister), Istanbul, Abdullah Freres

Surrender of the fortress of Nikopol, July 4, 1877
(Nikolai Dmitriev-Orenburgsky)

THE OTTOMAN-RUSSIAN WAR (THE WAR OF '93)

Relations were suspended after the proposals made at the Shipyard Conference were rejected and the ambassadors of European states left Istanbul. Meanwhile, peace was made with Serbia. However, Montenegro's rebellion was continuing. The turmoil in Bosnia Herzegovina and the unrest in Bulgaria and Crete were not over.

In order to find a solution to this situation, a conference was held in London between England, France, Russia, Germany, Austria-Hungary and Italy as a result of the proposal of Britain and the Russian ambassador Ignatyev. A protocol has been signed in some of the Balkan states to accept the reform of the Porte, while the Ottoman borders are bound to be guaranteed by the great powers.

According to the protocol, two districts affiliated with the flag of Hersek populated by Christian people would be given to Montenegro and the Russian and Turkish troops in the Danube region would be reduced to the level of peace. Russia adopted this protocol. However, when the Sublime Porte rejected all requests the deal was off.

Count Nikolai Pavlovich Ignatiev

1877-78 Russo-Turkish War, scene from a battlefield

On April 23, 1877, the Russian acting chief of mission announced that political relations between the two states had been severed and left the country. The following day, Russian Chief Deputy Gorchakov issued a note to our acting chief of mission in Petersburg, Tevfik Bey that Russia had declared war against the Ottoman Empire. Furthermore, he also informed the ambassadors in Berlin, Vienna, Paris, London and Rome.

When the news of the war arrived in Istanbul in the afternoon on April 24th, Sultan Abdulhamid II ordered the European states to mediate for peace and send telegrams. He was strictly opposed to war. However, Midhat Pasha had previously conditioned the people and state dignitaries to war and made the war with Russia inevitable.

By the time the declaration of war of the Russians had arrived at the Porte, the Tsar's armies had already started to attack the homeland and the borders of Anatolia.

This war, called the war of '93 because it coincided with the Julian calendar year 1293 (fiscal), lasted nine months until the Edirne Armistice.

The telegram from Tevfik Bey and the declaration of war was read in the parliament session gathered on 25 April, and speeches were made against Russia.

Russian Emperor, Alexander II

On the other hand, European states France, Italy, Britain and Austria declared their neutrality. Russia's declaration of war against the Ottoman Empire worried the British. Britain was worried that Istanbul which was a commercial center with strategic importance would fall into the hands of the Russians, the danger of Egypt and Suez, the Indian road and the loss of free passage in the Danube and the Straits would be gone at the end of the war. Collateral on these issues was demanded from Russia. Otherwise, they would reconsider their neutrality. Russia immediately provided the necessary guarantees to the UK.

The Russians crossed the Danube with a force of 40,000. This, in a sense, meant losing the war. The only natural obstacle was the Balkan Mountains. It would be very difficult to stop the Russians until Edirne, even to Istanbul, if they succeeded in crossing the mountains.

The Russian armies occupied Tărn ovo and Nikopol and seized the Shipka pass over the Balkan Mountains. The Russians who had achieved successive successes had to restrain Pleven in order to advance. Osman Pasha, a young commander, quickly set sail from Vidin and reached Pleven before the Russians and took defensive measures.

Suez Canal

On the other hand, young Marshal Süleyman Pasha came to the shores of western Thrace by sea with his corps. From there he reached the southern outskirts of the Shipka Pass. The Russian army suffered an unanticipated defeat in front of Pleven. They had to retreat. The Russians, who gathered strength in Pleven and sent their most experienced generals here, suffered a greater defeat in their second offensive. Osman Pasha's military forces was half of the Russians, their cannons were one third less in number. Suddenly the name of Osman Pasha became a household word in the world.

The bloodiest battles of the '93 War would have taken place in front of Pleven. The Russian Czar had come to the front in Pleven. The Romanian king was sought for help on behalf of Christianity. The attack was again repulsed by Osman Pasha. In the meantime, the number of Russian cannons had reached seven times that of the Pleven. The civilian men of Pleven, even the women, were involved in the defense. The Russian attack, which lasted 12 hours, resulted in defeat once again.

Gazi Osman Pasha resisted the much more superior Russian forces in front of Pleven for months and would go down in history. The arrival of the Russians in Istanbul was only possible after the fall of Pleven. Thousands of soldiers were crushed by cold and starvation during these wars. Civilian people were massacred.

The hero of the defensive fight taken place in Pleven

Ahmed Mukhtar Pasha

Like in Rumelia, there was serious resistance on the eastern front. The commander-in-chief Ahmad Mukhtar Pasha took Dogubeyazit and Ardahan and defeated the Russians who were advancing on Kars at the battle of Halyaz. There was no chance of success on the Eastern front against the increasing number of Russian troops. Ahmed Mukhtar Pasha left Kars and retreated to Erzurum in order not to damage his army further.

Sultan Abdulhamid gave the title of 'Ghazi' (veteran) to Osman Pasha, who repelled the Pleven attack and Ahmed Mukhtar Pasha who won the Gedikler victory. These pashas were known as national heroes until the end of their lives. Ahmed Mukhtar Pasha would become the commissioner of Egypt and grand vizier after the Constitutional Monarchy while Ghazi Osman Pasha would serve as the Minister of Defense and the chief of council

THE SOLE ADMINISTRATOR

SHUTTING DOWN THE ASSEMBLY

The armistice of Edirne, which ended the war, was signed on January 31, 1878. The western states, worried about the progress of the Russians, were concerned that their interests would be in jeopardy. Abdulhamid II got cognizant of the interests of Western states when the '93 War ended and expressed the idea of applying a policy of balance to the assembly which had convened at the palace as follows:

"I didn't want the war. A number of adventurers wanted it and they dragged the nation after them. As you see, we are defeated. Our position is clear. Now, the main issue is to take advantage of the competition and remain standing."

A knowledgeable statesman Ahmed Wafik Pasha

Sultan Hamid, in his early days on the throne

Meanwhile, Sultan Ahmed Hamdi Pasha was dismissed (4 February 1878) and Ahmed Wafik Pasha was appointed as grand vizier. There were fierce discussions in the post-war parliament. Instead of thinking about the interests of the state by gathering under the umbrella of a single state, the MPs adopted a separatist manner, either for their own personal ambition or as the spokesperson of the groups they represented. In addition, some of the MPs held the Sultan responsible for the war and as a result of presumptuous speeches Sultan Abdulhamid concluded that the constitution administration was not beneficial to the country. Based on the authority granted by the constitutional law, the sultan closed the assembly indefinitely and took over the administration (February 13, 1878).

TREATY OF SAN STEFANO

The Russians established headquarters in Yeşilköy after the treaty. The treaty to be signed had some serious conditions such as the establishment of a Bulgarian Principality to include Western Thrace, East Thrace up to Kirklareli and Macedonia; handing Nish over to Serbia, leaving Dobruja to Romania, expanding the borders of Montenegro, handing over Batumi, Kars Ardahan, Dogubeyazit and 6 navy battleships to Russia as war compensation. Sultan Abdulhamid did not accept to give the battleships. However, on March 3, 1878, the 29-point San Stefano Treaty was signed with Russia, but it never entered into force.

Yeşilköy or the 'Gare de San-Stefano'

Russia did not want the big states to be involved. This treaty allowed Russia to gain a lot of influence in the Balkans because of the status it had enforced regarding Bulgaria. This disrupted the political balance between states.

Sultan Abdulhamid Han did not accept this treaty which had serious consequences. Seeing that the Indian pathway was in danger, Britain wanted the San Stefano treaty to be discussed at an international conference on the grounds that it violated the Paris Treaty. In addition, the UK was planning to seize some concessions from the Ottomans under the excuse of supporting the Ottoman Empire at this conference.

THE ÇIRAĞAN INCIDENT

In the meantime an unexpected coup attempt took place. The journalist and scholar Ali Suavi wanted to overthrow Sultan Hamid and replace him with Murad V who was showing signs of recovery and to have a voice in government himself. Ali Suavi, who was a former Jeune-Turk and who later praised Abdulhamid in his articles, raided the Ciragan Palace in order to put Sultan Murad back on the throne (May 20, 1878). Ali Suavi was an adventurous, breezy yet unbalanced person. Although he was well educated, his political ambitions were overwhelming.

A rebel with turban, Ali Suavi

At the time of the incident, Britain promised to be allowed the occupation of the island of Cyprus, to make reforms in the eastern provinces after peace, and that the European states would intervene in the serious situation that the Ottoman State faced in its favor. In this atmosphere, the Ottoman government would be obliged to ask the British for help against the Russians who would possibly benefit from an incident incurring in Istanbul. Such turmoil could be stirred by someone who was pro-British, someone who did not think of the consequences of his actions and was an outrageous adventurer. In this respect, Ali Suavi was an invaluable element.

Mahmud Jalaleddin Pasha
(Prince Sabahattin on his left and Lutfullah Beg on his right)

The calamity of the '93 war and the Russian army going all the way to Yeşilköy had already created a vacuum. Ali Suavi tricked several hundred people fleeing Rumelia and put them on barges and landed at Çırağan Palace. While he was trying to get Murad V out of the palace with his assistant Nişli Salih, Beşiktaş Guard Yedisekiz Hasan Pasha was informed of the incident and he killed Ali Suavi with a stick in his hand. 23 of the immigrants were killed and the others surrendered. Sultan Murad and his mother were transferred to the Malta Pavilion that day, and were kept under surveillance for some time.

In fact, it was understood that the incident was not merely the doing of one ambitious man and migrants, it also involved members of the army. In addition to Damad Mahmud Pasha and Mehmed Sâdık Pasha, it was discovered that British and Russian agents were also involved in this organization. As a result, it was realized that this incident, which at first glance seemed like a mad attempt, was actually a highly studied operation.

This coup attempt, which was suppressed in a short time, sent Abdulhamid into deep thought. The Grand vizier and the Chamberlain were dismissed. The fact that statesmen and foreign states were so influential in the country necessitated the sultan to be more cautious for the nation and the peace of the country. Therefore, in order to be able to follow the movements of internal and external enemies closely, the Teşkilat-ı Mahsusa (Special Organization) detective organization which is commensurate with the current intelligence organization was established. Thanks to this intelligence agency, what was happening in every corner of the country was reported to him on a day by day basis. Hundreds of people would be assigned to this task.

As a matter of fact, Sultan Abdulhamid stated that 'he had founded this organization not to spy on citizens but to get to know and follow those who betrayed the state even though they were paid from the treasury and up to their gills with the blessing of the Ottomans.'

BRITISH DOMINANCE IN CYPRUS

The San Stefano Treaty intimidated major European states. With its coming into force, Russian influence would be greatly increased. Furthermore, with Bulgaria's independence and expansion of territory meant that the Russians could easily descend on the Mediterranean. This made Britain, Austria and Germany uncomfortable. States that had signed the 1856 Paris Treaty decided to convene a congress in Berlin instead of the provisional San Stefano Treaty.

Government officials around Yeşilköy

Meanwhile the Istanbul Treaty was made between England and Turkey (June 4, 1877). According to the treaty, the administration of Cyprus would be left to Britain, the island would remain legally bound to Turkey, surplus income from administrative revenue would be sent to Istanbul. In return, Britain would support Turkey in Berlin in the conference and alleviate the severe conditions of the San Stefano treaty. The British occupation would continue until the Russians returned Kars and Ardahan to the Ottoman State, and if this happened, the British would immediately withdraw from Cyprus. But this would not be the case. Abdulhamid Han agreed to this treaty in desperation. This treaty meant the end of the three hundred years of Turkish rule in Cyprus.

THE BERLIN CONFERENCE AND ITS CONSEQUENCES

With the positive results of the Turco-British alliance, the states of Britain, France, Germany, Austria, Turkey, Italy and Russia signed the agreement at the Berlin Congress, which was chaired by German Prime Minister Prince Bismark (13 July 1878).

According to the agreement, Kars, Ardahan and Artvin were left to Russia. Dobruja was given to Romania, Nish to Serbia, Thessaly to Greece, the administration of Bosnia Herzegovina and Yenipazar was left to Austria-Hungary and the administration of Cyprus was handed over to Britain. The legal ties of principalities of Montenegro, Romania, Serbia with the

Drawing shows car and person on street near walled compounds, Tunisia

Napoleon III's surrender to Bismarck

Ottomans were severed and these states became completely independent. The Eastern Principality of Rumelia was established with close ties with the Principality of Bulgaria, which had extensive privileges. In addition, France had prepared the occupation of Tunisia during the conference. Indeed, the French troops occupied Tunisia with an excuse on May 12, 1881. When the governor could not get the help he wanted, he signed a document that left Tunisia's protection to the French. The Istanbul government never recognized the actual status as legal. The 310-year-old Ottoman State administration in Tunisia had thus come to an end.

At the end of this war, the Ottoman State suffered a loss of five and a half million inhabitants and 212 thousand square kilometers of land. This does not include the loss of places such as Tunisia, Cyprus, Bulgaria, Bosnia Herzegovina. Moreover, the Ottoman state would pay 800 million gold francs war reparations to Russia, and incur improvements in East Anatolia in regions where the Armenian population was dense as well as in Macedonia.

A new political balance was established in Europe and especially in the Balkans. The signed document showed that the Ottoman statesmen were inadequate and aroused discontent in Russia and Romania. The Russians were unable to find what they were hoping for their great losses and sacrifices.

Mediterranen (G. Eric and Edith Matson Photograph Collection)

The war compensation was paid in installments during the reign of Sultan Abdulhamid. The sultan refrained from implementing the article regarding the improvements regarding the Armenians and Macedonia for a long time.

According to the Berlin treaty, three independent states emerged in the Balkans such as Serbia, Montenegro and Romania.

Sultan Abdulhamid II took the necessary lessons from the catastrophic results of the 1877-78 war, which he entered without his will. He would follow a highly cautious and prudent policy throughout his administration and prevent the state from entering another war.

THE DEATH OF SULTAN AZIZ IN YILDIZ COURT

Five years had passed since the murder of Sultan Aziz. The trial of the defendants began. Among them were Midhat and Mahmud Jalaleddin, Mütercim Rushdi, Damad Nuri Pashas.

The case was filed with the official notification of Pervinfelek Hanım, a former concubine from the palace and the wife of Münir Bey (Pasha). Such a case should have been heard in a regular court, however it was heard in Yıldız Court established in tent erected next to Malta Pavilion in Yıldız.

Although a neutral and fair committee of judges had been appointed, images such as the trial being held near the palace, the frequent contact of the pashas with the judges, was a matter of criticism especially in the European press. At the end of the three-day hearings, the court sentenced nine people to death, and two suspects were sentenced to prison terms. These penalties were also endorsed by appeal and religious authorities

Midhat Pasha was the most well known among those who were tried in court and found guilty and convicted. Pasha was expelled in 1877 and although he had no official duty, he carried out various political negotiations in Europe and especially in London and consequently was allowed to return to the country and live in Crete. He was pardoned by the sultan in 1880, taking into account his successful service in the provinces he was first appointed to Syria and then to the governor's office of Izmir.

Midhat Pasha, who was informed about the decision of arrest in the trial, fled from his house where he was at night and took shelter in the French consulate in Izmir. However, on the pressure of the government, the French Ministry of Foreign Affairs gave instructions to the Izmir consul and ordered that the pasha is delivered to the Turkish authorities. Subsequently, Midhat Pasha was arrested and brought to Istanbul by ferry.

Despite the court's ruling for execution, Abdulhamid Han was not in favor of bloodshed. A council of 25 leading statesmen convened and the rulings were presented for their views. The majority of Parliament was in favor of executing the penalties.

None of the criminals sentenced to death for murder were executed. Sultan Abdulhamid exercised the right given to him by the caliphate and showed mercy to the criminals sentenced to death and sent them into exile.

Crete

THE BRITISH OCCUPY EGYPT

The Egyptian Khedive Ismail Pasha borrowed a large amount of money from the UK and France, and could not pay the interest of the debt, which was 100 million in British currency. When the debts could not be paid, Britain and France applied pressure to initiate various financial measures. More than half of the shares of the Suez Canal in the hands of Ismail Pasha were transferred to Britain. In addition, a Frenchman and a British controller entered the Egyptian cabinet. The new deputies reduced the number of Egyptian troops and dismissed approximately 2,500 officers from the army. The officers rebelled against Khedive Ismail Pasha under the leadership of Miralay Urabi Bey.

When Egypt became chaotic, Abdulhamid II removed Ismail Pasha and replaced him with his son Tevfik Pasha (25 June 1879). Urabi was promoted to brigadier and given the title of 'pasha'. Urabi Pasha terminated the tasks of the European deputies in Egypt and sent them to their homelands. Before long, France and England sent two fleets to Alexandria. After the foreign fleets appeared at the port, attacks started on the homes of Europeans. When the turmoil reached this level, the British navy opened fire on Alexandria. Subsequently the British occupied Cairo. After a while Urabi Pasha was captured and exiled to Ceylon (Srilanka).

At this point the Ottoman rule in Egypt had remained on paper. Egypt was under British occupation and control by nominally staying under Ottoman rule and paying taxes.

Urabi Pasha

FINANCIAL SECURITY WAS ACHIEVED WITH THE PUBLIC DEBT ADMINISTRATION

The financial difficulties in recent years have also led to other problems with a political dimension and the reputation of the state has been damaged. Everything needs to be confiscated because of the external debts.

The state had undertaken a serious debt as of the late days of Sultan Abdulaziz. As a solution to the problems experienced after the Crimean War, firstly, on June 28, 1855, a five article agreement was made in London and five million British gold coins were borrowed from Britain and France. The accumulated debts through the following years amounted to 5 billion 297 million 676 thousand 500 francs.

Abdulhamid II who took over the state in debt, agreed to pay a delegation comprised of Ottoman Bank representatives and a delegation of Galata bankers 1 million 350 thousand pounds per annum in external debt with Rüsum-ı Sitte (Six Taxes) called Muskirat (Intoxicants), consisting of Fish, Salt, Silk, Tobacco and Stamp revenue proceeds. This delegation would uphold these taxes.

In addition to the six types of taxes determined for the payment of debts, Düyûn-ı Umûmiye (Public Debt) Administration was established as collateral to the taxes of Cyprus and the Eastern Rumelia. As a result of this stable stance, the principal and accrued interest debt of 252 million 801 thousand 885 Ottoman liras was reduced to 106 million 437 thousand 234 lira. Representatives of foreign creditor countries participated in this organization, which was extended to include all external debts. The Sultan invited all foreign creditors to Istanbul. The subsequent negotiations concluded in an agreement which was reached on December 20, 1881.

Public Debts Office, the still standing building

This decision was published in the month of Muharram (28 Muharram 1299), therefore it is also called Muharram Decree.

Thanks to the agreements and commitments, nearly three-fifths of the debts were deleted. The financial credibility of the state was reinstated and foreign intervention and political attrition were prevented.

Sultan Hamid described the negligence of statesmen which had continued for years as follows:

"Our exalted uncle Sultan Abdülaziz Holiness, may he rest in Heaven, has left all state affairs in the hands of honorable individuals who had gained a reputation for their knowledge and wisdom in Istanbul, such as Âlî, Fuad, Mahmud, Hüseyin Avni and Midhat Pashas. They accepted whatever has been said; they have taken many loans for the rebuilding of the country. While they were signing for these loans they have taken their percentage. (...) As a result, the state is immersed in debt and a large part of its revenues is paid toward the debt - that is, even if a small stamp is issued for the cleanliness of the city, if a new revenue collection is attempted, according to the treaties the Düyûn-ı Umumiye will be endeavoring to take it.

"If the coins these wise men took had stayed in their families, they would constitute a bank today or a great concession in the country that would use a part of the population in place to generate wealth in the country and support small scale tradesmen and small national banks could be established.

"However, with the easy come easy go mentality, the bribes that they took and handed over to the wine merchant Azarians and Lorandos for safekeeping portrayed these accounts erroneously and although they were wealthy, on their demise most of the family and relatives claimed that there was no money for the burial and because of these petitions, the charges were countered by the Imperial Treasury."[1]

1 Devlet ve Memleket Görüşlerim (My Views on the State and the Country), v. 1, (Ed.) A. Atilla Çetin, p. 14-15, Çamlıca Basım Yayın, Istanbul 2011.

REBELLION STARTS

BULGARIAN REBELLION IN EAST RUMELIA

The Bulgarian prince did not hesitate in carrying out the campaign, either open or clandestine, of annexing the Eastern Rumelia province to Bulgaria. Bulgaria's Gavril Pasha was appointed to replace the governor of the eastern Rumelia province, which was established following the decision taken in the Congress of Berlin. Shortly afterward, Gavril Pasha was arrested by the militia forces and the unification of Bulgaria and Eastern Rumelia (18 September 1885) was announced. The Bulgarian forces built up along the Ottoman border.

Italian political cartoon depicting the sides taking part in the Congress of Berlin

This was a rebellion because Bulgaria was a principality under the Ottoman Empire. This was also contrary to the Berlin Treaty. That's why the Sublime Porte was entitled to take military action. However, they chose not to do so and sent a protesting note to European states. Necessary measures against the possibility of a Bulgarian offensive were taken.

The European states remained passive despite the violation of the Berlin Treaty and the application of the Sublime Porte. According to England and Austria, a large Bulgaria, which would not be under the tutelage of Russia, would not be a problem. Thus, the progress and settlement of Russian influence in the Balkans would be prevented.

At the end of the negotiations, the eastern Rumelian province was left to Bulgaria, however a Bulgarian Prince was appointed as leader. The province would continue to pay taxes to the Ottoman Empire and Kardzhali and Ropchoz would remain with Turkey.

THE GREECE OPERATION

Meanwhile, sensing the weakness of the Ottoman state, Greece, with the support of Europe, began to take action to get Crete. Thessaly and Narda had been given to Greece after the '93 war. Greece did not find this adequate and set its eyes on Ioannina and Crete. The Etniki Eterya *(Society of Friends)* that wanted to take Crete inside its borders prevailed in domestic politics in Greece. With the support of the Cretan committee in Athens, blood was shed on the island, and the Greeks were spreading propaganda that the Christians in Crete were being annihilated. European major states sent battleships into Crete waters.

On January 21, 1886, the Sublime Porte sent a note to the Greek government and a navy to the island. The Greeks had begun to advance in Ottoman territory. France then sent an ultimatum to Greece. Meanwhile, the Greek armies were thrashed by Ahmed Eyub Pasha and forced beyond the border.

The Ottoman army, under the control of the military commander (Marshal) Edhem Pasha in Elassona, soon advanced into Greece. In a short time like a month, the Greek army lost many positions and retreated to Thessaly. The Tirhala-Çatalca line, which Europeans said could not be crossed in six months, was crossed in a few days. Ottoman troops defeated the Greek army in front of Domekos. They were 150 kilometers from Athens and the road was open. Sultan Abdulhamid was awarded the title of 'Ghazi 'on May 26, 1897 upon this victory.

The Western states and the Russian Czar, who were worried that Greece would be taken back by the Ottomans, sent a telegraph to Is-

Alexander Ypsilantis

tanbul to reach an understanding. The first talks between the states acting on behalf of Greece and the Sublime Porte started on 3 June in Istanbul in the Tophane pavilion. Two sessions per week were held for 3 months and 16 days, and finally on 18 September 1897 an agreement was reached.

The following decisions were reached at the peace conference in Istanbul:

1- Thessaly occupied by the Turkish army would be returned to Greece, some changes in favor of Turkey would take place on the border.

2- Greece would pay Turkey 4 million Ottoman gold coins as compensation as well as 100 thousand Ottoman gold coins to pay for losses incurred by Turkish nationals.

3. Border gangs and banditry will be prohibited along the border, reciprocal mail and telegraph communication would be re-established, criminals will be returned and trade and navigation will be free.

4- The capitulation boundaries that Greece benefited from will be narrowed.

According to the provisions of the agreement, the Ottoman army seems to have been defeated, while Greece was almost certainly defeated and lost practically nothing.

The Ottoman army gained the prestige it had lost and manifested that it had maintained its power in the Ottoman-Greek War.

AUTONOMY TO CRETE

There was no mention of Crete in the treaty of the war over the island. That is because the states decided on this matter in advance. As a matter of fact, the autonomy of Crete was proclaimed just two weeks after signing the peace treaty on 18 December 1897. Britain, France, Russia and Italy agreed among themselves and established a new regime. The island of Crete had become a neutral and autonomous province under Ottoman dominance. A Christian governor whom the states considered appropriate would be appointed by the Sultan for five years. An elected assembly, in which Muslims would be represented, would be formed. As the security of Muslims was ensured, the Ottoman military would withdraw from the island. Crete was to give an annual tax to the Ottoman treasury.

It was now time to connect the island formally with Greece. This didn't take too long. First, the second son of the Greek king (George I), Prince George, was appointed by the states to Crete. Subsequently, the withdrawal of Ottoman troops was asserted on the grounds that there were no Greek soldiers on the island. Greece, which had just come out of the war, included Crete into its own borders, albeit unofficially. In the face of the threat of war by the great states, the Sublime Porte had to recognize this autonomy and lost all influence on the island.

ARMENIAN OPERATIONS START

The engineering of the Armenians in the Ottoman Empire began with the Reforms. There was no 'Armenian issue' until 1878. Armenians were one of the loyal, approved and industrious nations of the state. Because they were highly trusted at the state level, they were assigned to the most important positions. There were many Armenians as district governor, governor and judge. In addition, they had acquired significant civil servant positions in the Chamberlain and the Sublime Porte. They included viziers and ministers. They served the state loyally. They had complete freedom in the Ottoman country and their social institutions were active freely.

After the success of the Russians in the War of 93, the article regarding 'improvement in Eastern Anatolian province' was included in the

Sivas as a melting point for cultures and ethnicities; an Armenian, Kurdish and Turkish women featured (Right to left)

Berlin Conference, an Armenian movement provoked by Russia and supported by the British would begin. This was certainly not a coincidence. Together with the Reforms, the Armenian patriarchs started to organize the Armenians, and the organizations that started as charities evolved into gangs. The Hinchak (sound of chimes) Committee, which was headquartered in Switzerland, and subsequently the Dashnak (Union) Committee, which separated from them, aimed to establish an independent Armenia in the Ottoman geography. They generated rebellion in place to this end.

The Russians implemented policies on the Armenians early on. They wanted to Russianize and Orthodoxize the Armenians in the South Caucasus and Eastern Anatolia.

Britain, like the Russians, had their designs on the Armenians. They demanded that the reforms foreseen by Article 61 of the Berlin treaty be honored and supported the Hinchaks. In other words, they wanted Eastern Anatolia to fall into the situation of Lebanon, Bulgaria and Crete. Sultan Abdulhamid would never put this article into practice

The Hinchaks had set their eyes on Anatolia for "Armenia". They had set their eyes on the six provinces which were called Vilâyat-ı Sitte, i.e., the administrative establishment at that time as Erzurum, Van, Diyarbakır, Sivas, Bitlis and Mamuretü'l-Aziz (Kharput) (This area includes all of Erzurum, Erzincan, Van, Ağrı, Hakkâri, Muş, Bitlis, Siird, Diyarbakır, Elazığ, Mardin, Bingöl, Malatya, Sivas, Amasya, Tokat and partly Giresun provinces). This wide area, consisting of a part of Eastern and Central Anatolia, was more than one third of the Anatolian continent. However, the Armenians were not a majority anywhere. These provinces were a geographical, racial and historical part of the Turkish homeland, which constituted the basis of the Ottoman State. This prompted Sultan Hamid to say to the envoy next to him on an expedition to Germany that 'I would rather die than accept reforms that make the Eastern Anatolia autonomous!'

The Armenians lived as both a small minority in the six provinces as well as in a dispersed way. Moreover, the Armenian middle class in the empire was completely foreign to these ideas and purposes. Most of the people were indifferent to the activities of the committee, even informed on them. Hence, many rich Armenians were killed by the Hunchaks.

Abdulhamid saw the Armenian game and thought about using Russia as a trump card against Britain's policy based on interest. He vigorously refused to carry out reforms in the provinces occupied by Armenians. He knew that any reforms would ultimately mean autonomy and even an independent administration. Greece, Serbia, Romania, Montenegro, Bulgaria, Samos, Lebanon and Crete were examples of this.

A cavalry troop of the Hamidie Regiment in Ourfa (Servet-i Fünun, No. 115)

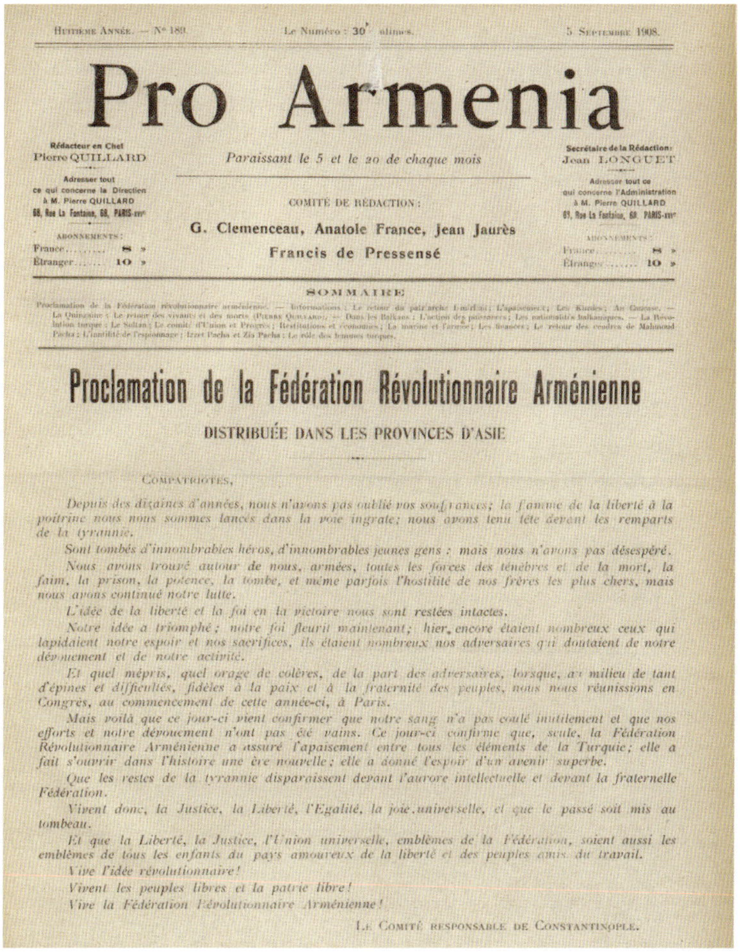

Huitième Année. — N° 189. Le Numéro : 30 centimes. 5 Septembre 1908.

Pro Armenia

Rédacteur en Chef
Pierre QUILLARD

Adresser tout ce qui concerne la Direction à M. Pierre QUILLARD
68, Rue La Fontaine, 68, PARIS-XVIe

ABONNEMENTS :
France........ 8 »
Étranger...... 10 »

Paraissant le 5 et le 20 de chaque mois

COMITÉ DE RÉDACTION :

G. Clemenceau, Anatole France, Jean Jaurès
Francis de Pressensé

Secrétaire de la Rédaction :
Jean LONGUET

Adresser tout ce qui concerne l'Administration à M. Pierre QUILLARD
68, Rue La Fontaine, 68, PARIS-XVIe

ABONNEMENTS :
France........ 8 »
Étranger...... 10 »

SOMMAIRE

Proclamation de la Fédération révolutionnaire arménienne. — Informations : Le retour du patriarche Izmirlian; L'apaisement; Les Kurdes; Au Caucase. — La Quinzaine : Le retour des vivants et des morts (Pierre Quillard). — Dans les Balkans : L'action des puissances; Les nationalités balkaniques. — La Révolution turque : Le Sultan; Le comité d'Union et Progrès; Restitutions et économies; La marine et l'armée; Les finances; Le retour des cendres de Mahmoud Pacha; L'inutilité de l'espionnage; Izzet Pacha et Zia Pacha; Le rôle des femmes turques.

Proclamation de la Fédération Révolutionnaire Arménienne

DISTRIBUÉE DANS LES PROVINCES D'ASIE

Compatriotes,

Depuis des dizaines d'années, nous n'avons pas oublié vos souffrances; la flamme de la liberté à la poitrine nous nous sommes lancés dans la voie ingrate; nous avons tenu tête devant les remparts de la tyrannie.

Sont tombés d'innombrables héros, d'innombrables jeunes gens : mais nous n'avons pas désespéré.

Nous avons trouvé autour de nous, armées, toutes les forces des ténèbres et de la mort, la faim, la prison, la potence, la tombe, et même parfois l'hostilité de nos frères les plus chers, mais nous avons continué notre lutte.

L'idée de la liberté et la foi en la victoire nous sont restées intactes.

Notre idée a triomphé; notre foi fleurit maintenant; hier, encore étaient nombreux ceux qui lapidaient notre espoir et nos sacrifices, ils étaient nombreux nos adversaires qui doutaient de notre dévouement et de notre activité.

Et quel mépris, quel orage de colères, de la part des adversaires, lorsque, au milieu de tant d'épines et difficultés, fidèles à la paix et à la fraternité des peuples, nous nous réunissions en Congrès, au commencement de cette année-ci, à Paris.

Mais voilà que ce jour-ci vient confirmer que notre sang n'a pas coulé inutilement et que nos efforts et notre dévouement n'ont pas été vains. Ce jour-ci confirme que, seule, la Fédération Révolutionnaire Arménienne a assuré l'apaisement entre tous les éléments de la Turquie; elle a fait s'ouvrir dans l'histoire une ère nouvelle; elle a donné l'espoir d'un avenir superbe.

Que les restes de la tyrannie disparaissent devant l'aurore intellectuelle et devant la fraternelle Fédération.

Vivent donc, la Justice, la Liberté, l'Egalité, la joie universelle, et que le passé soit mis au tombeau.

Et que la Liberté, la Justice, l'Union universelle, emblèmes de la Fédération, soient aussi les emblèmes de tous les enfants du pays amoureux de la liberté et des peuples amis du travail.

Vive l'idée révolutionnaire!

Vivent les peuples libres et la patrie libre!

Vive la Fédération Révolutionnaire Arménienne!

Le Comité responsable de Constantinople.

Proclamation of the Revolutionary Armenian Federation seen on a pro-Armenian paper issued in Paris

Abdulhamid Han, who knew which way the wind was blowing started to establish 'Hamidiye Regiments' from the Muslim tribes in Eastern Anatolia in order to ensure peace in the region. With the establishment of the Hamidiye Regiments, the following was aimed: to take advantage of the tribes included in the military discipline as the law enforcement officers for Eastern Anatolia, to create regular cavalry units, to create a ready-made force against a possible Russian occupation, to straighten out the elements that were open to external instigation and rebellion, settle the clans and civilize them; to educate and discipline them, to end the tribal feuds, to use all the potential in the region in favor of the state and take this opportunity to build roads, bridges, school buildings etc. and reconstruct East Anatolia. The Hamidiye Regiments would provide great benefit in the years to come, during and after the world war.

After a while, the Hunchak committee was divided into two. The Trockak (the Flag), who left, were pro-Russian unlike the Hunchaks and they believed that the Armenian ideal could only be realized with the help of the Russians. They immediately wanted to reach their ambitions by taking action and creating havoc. The Trockak subsequently adopted the name of Dashnak. Armenian officers and members of the resistance movement most of who had been trained and tasked in the Russian army were preparing for armed combat.

In time, the Armenian people of the Ottoman Empire began to lose their former popularity and credibility with the Ottoman Empire, who saw the middle class and the very rich Armenians cooperating with the committees, either willingly or under coercion. For this reason many Armenian schools were closed. Many churches were searched by government forces because of information that weapons, ammunition and bombs were hid by the revolutionaries.

The first major event would take place in Sasun district. In the new tax year, the Armenians did not want to pay taxes because of the governor who had imposed an erroneous tax the previous year. The tax collectors who went to the villages were met with arms. Finally the government had to deploy troops there. Then the Armenians, on the instructions of the committees, burned their villages and towns and retreated to the mountains.

Armenian families and the innocent that were certainly safe during the clashes occured between the Armenian rebels and the Ottoman security forces

Queen Victoria in her early years

At the same time, they spread the news that Ottoman troops had destroyed the villages and towns and massacred the people. Hunchak and Trochak committees made propaganda throughout Europe and even America to the tune of 'the Turks are slaughtering Christians'.

At the end of the events, the British wanted to intervene in the committees. England took Russia and France in tow and attempted to get autonomy for Erzurum from the Sublime Porte by demanding reform. Although the Sublime Porte did not take this demand into consideration, the representatives of the UK, France and Russia had to be included in the established investigation committee.

The investigation commission visited Muş and made the necessary investigations. While the European side was making accusatory statements against the Ottomans, it was revealed that the San Stefano and Berlin treaties and the British attitude had prepared these events. In spite of this, the three states presented a memorandum to the Sublime Porte on 11 May 1895. This memorandum called for reform in the Eastern provinces as per the Berlin Treaty, five-year governors appointed to these provinces with the approval of the great states, the establishment of provincial councils with representation from all elements as well as the establishment of a gendarmerie organization, the regulation of judicial and financial affairs, the control of the movements of nomad tribes. The Ottoman state refused all these requests (June 3, 1895).

ARMENIAN REBELLION IS GROWING

After the rejection of the memorandum presented by the European states, an event called 'Armenian Incident' took place in Istanbul.

On September 30, 1895, the Armenians started a large scale demonstration for the fulfillment of the wishes in the memorandum. In this attempted rebellion headed by the Armenian Patriarch İzmirliyan, several hundred Armenians marched from Kadırga to Sultanahmed and from there to the Sublime Porte. When the Armenians endeavored to turn the march into an uprising and killed an Ottoman officer, the law enforcement tried to disperse the groups with firearms. More than a hundred Armenians died in the events that lasted until October 9th. Also police, gendarmerie and people were injured and killed.

Jerusalem, once a center for diverse beliefs and religious leaders

The Grand Vizier Said Pasha was dismissed and replaced with Kamil Pasha because he failed to take necessary measures and immediately suppress the uprising when the Armenian incident took place (1 October 1895). Kamil Pasha offered the sultan a memorandum concerning his powers. On this memorandum which surpassed all reason, the sultan dismissed Kamil Pasha and appointed Minister of Internal Affairs Halil Rifat Pasha (7 November 1895).

On August 26, 1896, the second largest Armenian incident, called the 'Bank Incident' took place in Istanbul. Some people, instigated by the committees, entered the Ottoman Bank one day under the pretext of business and suddenly started throwing things around. They took some of the officers as hostages and claimed that if the Armenian demands were not countered, they would blow up the bank with bombs. However, the government had been prepared for such situations ever since the first movement. The organization established by Abdulhamid II already had intelligence on the attempt. Law enforcement and troops were already positioned in the vicinity. This way, the event at the bank was immediately repressed and the perpetrators were arrested.

View of Galata and the (Imperial) Ottoman Bank, Constantinople (Abdullah Frères)

Halil Rifat Pasha, the then grand vizier (1895)

Nevertheless, the revolutionaries in the city were unable to calm down. They were attacking people, bombs, rifles and pistols were being fired from windows and many people, troops and police were killed. Before long, the patience of the Muslim people wore out. Both sides incurred losses. The police forces were trying to suppress the incidents and prevent the people from retaliation. In the meantime, the committees who had come from outside escaped on a French steamer, some even committed suicide. After all, the seeds of hostility between the Turks and Armenians who had lived with respect for each other's rights and freedoms had been planted.

On these events, the Trochak committee declared the Armenian demands to the European states. Sultan Abdulhamid decisively rejected these demands and requests for reforms for the six provinces. The Ottoman government issued a ruling on general amnesty, including the appointment of an Ottoman general inspectorate to the region and a proposal that Christians be appointed governors.

WORLD POLITICS

UNITED KINGDOM - GERMANY BALANCE

Abdulhamid Han was trying to strengthen the position of the state both inside and outside. He was aware of the ambitions of the world states on the vast geography of the ages-old empire. The emergence of nationalism was a great threat to the state, which included dozens of nations. In addition to the UK's plans in the Near East, their attitude regarding the Armenian issue distanced the Sublime Porte from Britain and moved it closer to Russia. However, in the course of time, as the Russian-Austrian proximity progressed, Sultan Abdulhamid felt obliged to lean towards German politics.

When the British saw how Sultan Abdulhamid's smart and cautious politics was linking the entire Islamic world to him, they concentrated their activities on the Ottoman Empire. On the one hand, while supporting the Committee of Union and Progress against the sultan, they were provoking the Bedouin tribes in the Arabian Peninsula and the Armenians in East Anatolia against the Ottoman State.

On the other hand, Sultan Abdulhamid was closely following the situation in Germany. When Germany established the national unity, world hegemony, political and economic influence and interest regions were already been divided among the other states. Germany viewed Britain as its greatest rival, and wanted to benefit from the loyalty of the Islamic realm to Abdulhamid as the Caliph and use it as an effective weapon against it. All colonial states, especially Britain, were disturbed by Germany's attitude.

In Germany, particularly under the influence of Prime Minister Otto von Bismarck, Kaiser Wilhelm I did not intend to participate actively in the Eastern Question. However, he also knew that British and French domination of the Near East should be restricted.

Italian political cartoon shows a map of Europe and the Near East at the end of the Russo-Turkish War, with most countries personified as human figures, the major exception being Russia which is a large octopus, followed by Greece as a crab nibbling at the right arm of "Turchia" who is being entangled by the tentacles of the octopus. (Grossi, Augusto, 1835-1919, artist.)

VRA RUSSA
ANNO VI.
RUSSIA
MAR NERO
ITERRANEO
PERSIA
CARTA
SERIO-COMICA
PEL
1878

Among the Islamic countries, India and Egypt were dominated by the British. The weapon used by Britain in response to the Caliphate and Islamism policy of the Kayser-Sultan cooperation, which led to them, was to fuel Arab nationalism and ideas of independence in Muslim countries under the Ottoman's sway. Yemen, Kuwait, Hejaz, Asir and Najid regions were the most suitable regions for these activities.

Kaiser Wilhelm I, who visited the Sultan two times during the later's reign

AS THE WORLD WAR IS APPROACHING

During the conference of the great states in Istanbul, Sultan Abdulhamid saw that their intention was not to guarantee the legal order of the Christian subjects as they had claimed, but initially to gain their autonomy and subsequently independence and destroy the Ottoman State. Thus, they would penetrate the administration of the disintegrating states as they wish and acquire new markets. Foreign states were instigating the Christian people in the country to rebel, putting pressure on the state by backing them as co-religionists. In addition, they wanted to establish a constitutional monarchy to break up the state among themselves and cause internal turmoil. They could easily find supporters for both purposes.

Some Turkish intellectuals did not realize that this type of administration was operable in national states and that in multinational bodies such as the Ottoman Empire it could be problematic and was instrumental for the plans of foreign states. Statesmen taking bribes were not only in ordinary state institutions, but even in the palace itself. The foreign state advocacy of some statesmen had become common knowledge. The Sultan saw all this, but could trust only a few people around him in this matter...

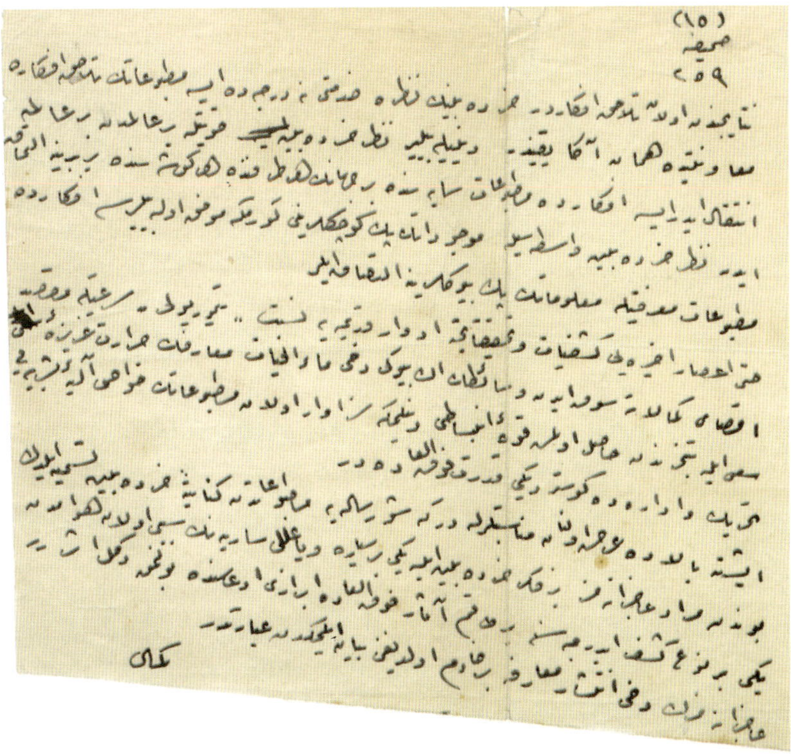

A piece of letter by Namık Kemal maintaining the function of the press for the public to be informed (Taha Toros Archive)

Europe's major states had decided to divide the world once and for all. The biggest goal was the Ottoman property. Sultan Hamid was aware that the state could not stand alone against these forces economically and militarily. Taking advantage of the rivalry between the countries, he followed a policy to make them play against each other by making one party believe that they would get a better deal. In the meantime, he was trying to make the Ottoman State strong in all respects.

As a matter of fact, the European balance, which was disrupted by the establishment of Germany, was about to make the big states fall over each other. The sultan was trying to keep his country alive until the colonial countries fell out with each other and subsequently join one of the groups when the conflict escalated. The sultan had avoided war for the 33 years he had spent on the throne, and pursued a policy of balance without getting close to any of the world's giants.

THE GERMAN IMPACT IN THE OTTOMAN ARMY

Radical innovations and changes in the Ottoman army began to take place in the period of Sultan Mahmud II after the lifting of the Janissary Corps in 1826. The Sultan was able to start to innovate after breaking the influence of the janissaries and some ulema, bureaucrats, military and other afflicted groups. Support had to be obtained from the developed countries of the period for the innovations and regulation arrangements in the military mechanism. Being aware of this, the sultan thought that the most appropriate thing to do was to invite the officers of Prussia which had a modern army for military arrangements. As a matter of fact, this intention was implemented in a short time.

In 1835 the King of Prussia III was requested for officers to consult for Ottoman army. In 1835-36 military experts such as Captain von Moltke, Lieutenant von Berg, Captain von Vinkle, Fischer and Mühlbach came to the country. Their main tasks were counseling on military matters and teaching in military schools. After completing their duties 1839, the officers returned home.

During the reigns of Sultan Abdulmejid and Abdulaziz, arrangements were made in the military organization for the modernization of the Turkish army. In the second half of the nineteenth century, within the framework of political relations of the period, officers of French origin employed as consultants in different units of the army. Some Prussian officers were also hired as advisors and teachers in military schools and associations in Istanbul during the same period

The reform-minded emperor, Sultan Mahmud II

Von Moltke while urging for attack to his fellow commander Hafiz Ahmed Pasha

From the 1840s onwards, the Ottoman army used a large amount of American weapons. Even in the first years of Sultan Abdulhamid II's rule, the sale of American weapons and materials was 90% of the total trade between the two countries. The Germans became superior in the competition between the US and German companies as of the 1870s.

German arms companies started to sell arms to the Ottoman Empire in the 1860s. In 1861, '63 and '64, German Krupp company received orders for cannon. After 1869, the company opened a representative office in Istanbul and Krupp cannon entered the Ottoman market more rapidly. After the 1877-78 Ottoman-Russian War in particular, Germany acquired a more influential position due to the political problems with Britain and France.

A gun manufactured by the German Krupp company in use by Turkish-Arab forces in 1911 during the Turco-Italian War

After 1881, Sultan Abdulhamid decided to engage in military cooperation with Germany to reorganize the Turkish army. The demand for a military delegation from Germany and the purchase of military supplies would gain momentum. In 1882, a German delegation of four, consisting of Infantry Captain Kamphövener, Artillery Captain von Hobe and Artillery Captain Ristow, led by Staff Col. Otto August Johannes Kaehler came to the Ottoman State. In the same year, ten young Turkish officers were sent to Germany to improve their education and training.

With the appointment of Colmar von der Goltz as major general to the leadership of the German reform group in the Ottoman army in 1886, the fortification of the Dardanelles and the Bosphorus against Britain and Russia brought to the agenda. The weapons needed for this reinforcement would come from Germany and, from Krupp in particular.

Kaiser Wilhelm II's visit to Istanbul in 1889 also served the German weapons industry and generated new orders. This visit of the German Kaiser had secured the sale of arms to Turkey with an average value of 15.3 million marks.

Colmar von der Goltz or Goltz Pasha, a Prussian Field Marshall

THE VISITS OF THE GERMAN EMPEROR

German Emperor Wilhelm II (1888-1918) came to the Ottoman lands three times in 1889, 1898 and 1917. During his first trip, each of the major European states had occupied a part of Ottoman territory. Russia had added Batumi, Kars and Ardahan to its territory. England had taken over Egypt, Austria had undertaken Bosnia and Herzegovina, France had Tunisia. Germany was not interested in occupying Ottoman territory and they had warm relations from the past. Moreover, the Germans were training the Ottoman army with the officers they sent in those years.

Wilhelm's visit was not just a friendly visit. Increasing German influence in the Ottoman territory and searching for markets for German goods were among the main objectives of the trip. For example on Emperor Wilhelm's first visit (1889) he managed to organize the large scale sale of German made mauser rifles to be used by the Ottoman army and on his second visit (1898) he ensured that the construction of the Baghdad Railway was commissioned to German companies.

Sultan Abdulhamid II was looking forward to this visit. Germany did not covet Ottoman territory and they had no colonies in Muslim countries.

State visit to Jerusalem by Wilhelm II of Germany, 1898

The sultan also planned to base his policy on the use of balance and interest relations with European states on Germany.

The emperor was greeted with a magnificent ceremony on his first visit to the empire on 2 November 1889 in Istanbul. The Emperor and his retinue, who had landed at Dolmabahce Palace continued to Yıldız Palace and settled in Şale Pavilion which had been prepared specially for them. They visited important places of Istanbul, observed the official parade of soldiers, held talks with the sultan, visited the Protestant church, the German Embassy and the German Hospital. On November 6, the German emperor and his retinue were sent off by the Turkish navy to Dardanelles (Çanakkale) as they had been welcomed.

German Emperor Wilhelm II's second visit would be more comprehensive and longer. The German navy carrying the Emperor and his entourage, anchored at the Dolmabahce front on Tuesday (October 18th). The German guests traveled from Dolmabahce to Yildiz, made a tour of the city, excursed through the city walls, and visited Beylerbeyi Palace, Camlica, Uskudar and the Anatolian shores of the Bosphorus. They went to Hereke by a special train from Haydarpasha where they visited the world-famous Hereke carpet factory. On the night of 22 October the emperor's fleet set off towards the Syrian coast under the protection of the Ottoman fleet accompanied by a volley of cannon fire that shook the port.

The German Embassy, Beyoglu (Istanbul)

On October 25, 1898, the German emperor arrived in Haifa; accompanied by special Ottoman soldiers, from there they travelled to Jerusalem on 29 October. In Jerusalem the Emperor visited the Church of Kamame, the German Consulate and went to Bethlehem. They attended the opening ceremony of the German Church (Erlöserkirche). They visited places such as Prophet David's tomb and mosque, Zeytindağı, Syria Orphanage. On Wednesday, November 2, 1898, the emperor traveled to the Harem-i Sharif area and visited the Qubbat as-Sakhrah and Masjid al-Aqsa with the Mufti of Jerusalem and the governor of Syria.

The Hamidieh Bastions built for the proper defense of the city

On Friday November 4, the emperor and the empress were sent off to Jaffa with an official ceremony. They traveled from there to Beirut and from there on November 7 by train to Damascus. The emperor visited the Umayyad Mosque in Damascus and the tomb of Salahaddin al-Ayyubi and made a speech stating that they were the friends of millions of Muslims in the world.

Wilhelm II's last visit to Turkey when Abdulhamid Han was living his final months in Beylerbeyi would coincide with the most critical phase of the First World War. The emperor had arrived by train to Istanbul via Bul-

Jerusalem from southeast, showing city walls, the Dome of the Rock, and al-Aqsa mosque

garia. On the morning of 15 October 1917, Sultan Mehmed Reşad (1909-1918) met the emperor at Sirkeci Railway Station. The emperor engaged in various visits and meetings in Istanbul, attended opening ceremonies, and visited the area where the Çanakkale battles had taken place.

German Emperor Wilhelm II's travels had caused major reverberations in the Turkish and the world press. It was instrumental in introducing Ottoman splendor, power and hospitality to the world. On the other hand, Sultan Abdulhamid knew how to use these visits which ensured Turkish-German rapprochement against states like the United Kingdom and Russia that wanted to break the Ottoman State asunder. Unfortunately, the members of the Committee of Union and Progress (CUP) who did not understand the politics of the sultan and could not carry out the politics of balance would lead the country into war with Germany and pave the way for the disintegration of the state.

THE POWER OF THE CALIPHATE

Sultan Hamid, who came to the throne in the most depressing times of the Ottoman State, highlighted the Caliphate organization, which had been held by the state for three and a half centuries to keep the state strong both inside and out.

Abdulhamid II aimed to realize serenity and solidarity by uniting the Ottoman nation around Islam, and to provide the necessary motivation for the progress of the state. Furthermore, he was pursuing an active policy of balance in the capacity of the patron of Muslims against the colonialist states of Europe, particularly Britain and Russia, which intervened on every part of the state and even on its future.

The British were worried about the interest of Muslims in the world for the Ottoman caliphate. After the British seized control of India in the 1840s and ended the Turkish state there, Iran, Afghanistan and the Ottoman Empire stood as the remaining independent Muslim states in the world. Muslims all across the globe wanted a spiritual leader, a strong state from which they hoped for help and protection. Since Afghanistan was under the influence of Russia, the Shiite Iranian state could not be unifying, the only power that was generally accepted was the Ottomans. Thus, Muslims in India, South East Asia, Central Asia and Africa addressed the Ottoman state and its caliphate.

The Sultan, who knew the influence of the Caliphate on millions of Muslims in Asia, Africa, the Hejaz region, sent scholars, sheikhs, and dervishes to educate Muslims and took care to associate them spiritually to the caliphate. He was trying to be in contact with Muslims all over the

William E. Gladstone standing on the balcony of a building where the windows are labeled 'Pride, Prestige, Supremacy in India, Commerce, British Empire, [and] Control of the Afgan Frontier'. On the ground is a thug identified as a 'Russian Rapscallion' who is about to throw a rock at Gladstone and the British Empire.

world in his capacity as the Caliph, raising his voice against the injustices and persecution suffered by Muslims. Even the sultanates in East Turkestan and Central Africa commissioned sermons to be made on his behalf, minted coins and were subjects to him.

The caliph had to solve disagreements between Muslim groups and be unifying. As a matter of fact, the dispute between Kuwait and Qatar, which was caused by the influence of the British and anti-Ottoman propaganda, was concluded without bloodshed with the involvement of the caliph. Furthermore, when members of the Islam Society in Liverpool were attacked during worship by some fanatic Brits, action was taken with the British government to ensure that necessary measures were taken.

The Sultan was closely following the Hejaz region. He was aware of the anti-Ottoman activities initiated by the British under the guise of research in Egypt and Arabia. The British had launched propaganda against the Ottomans among the Arabs. As a result of the British propaganda a debate had been instigated as to whether the head of the state had to be a descendant of Quraysh lineage. Since the Ottoman sultan would not be a legitimate caliph because he was not a descendant and therefore the Arabs needed to establish their own administrations, not be under the Ottoman rule. The Turks used Jamaladdin al-Afghani who claimed that the caliphate had been seized by the Turks and the Mecca was planning to announce Sharif Hussein as caliph. Abdulhamid II invited Afghani to Istanbul, kept

Bijâr Naşif Fortified station of the Hijaz Railway, 74 km north of Medina

Abdullah Quilliam, a convert in Liverpool

him closer and did not allow him to leave the country. The sultan commissioned scholars to give reply in a manner which would be satisfactory in scientific discussions and had booklets published.

British agents were working to spread Arab nationalism and claim the caliphate the Arabs' right, and to make the Egyptian Khedive the caliph. The Sultan responded to these efforts with the policy of Pan-Islamism. With the power given by the caliphate, he embarked on a religious crusade to ensure unity among Muslims. He benefited from the cult sheikhs and influential tribal chiefs. He sent experienced scholars and administrators to provinces with Muslim majorities, especially in Anatolia and Syria.

The Sultan was keeping a close eye on the Hejaz region. He had three main objectives in the idea of Pan-Islamism, also known as "İttihad-ı İslam": 1. Maintain the continuation of the regime, 2. Provide unity in the Islamic world, protecting Muslims, 3. Curb the crusader spirit and colonialism as much as possible.

With the power given to him by the caliphate, he even sent religious scholars to distant countries such as South Africa and Japan, and endeavored to spread Islam. The influence of the Sultan in China was so great that

A small building in Beijing as part of the Hamidie University established under the auspices of the Sultan

an Islamic university was opened in Beijing in his name and the Turkish flag fluttered at its gate. He commissioned the construction of the Hejaz railway extending from Damascus to Mecca and connected the holy lands to Istanbul. With counter-propaganda launched among the Arabs, he said that the common enemy was Western imperialism, the enemy of Islam, and that it had to be fought against.

When these efforts of the Sultan began to manifest results, the Western states would increase their pressure on the empire on the grounds that the non-Muslims were not equally treated.

UNPAID DEBTS AND THE OCCUPATION OF LESBOS

At the end of the reign of Sultan Abdulaziz, money was borrowed from two Frenchmen and this was also used to depose the sultan. The French filed a lawsuit for the debt that had not been paid for 15 years and won. As a major part of this money was used by Abdulaziz, nobody was able to burden Sultan Abdulhamid with the debt. Creditors, giving up a portion of interest notified that they would settle for 512 thousand lira.

Sultan Abdulhamid only learned about the matter after it became a political crisis. Nobody had the courage to talk about a debt that had been incurred with the intention of deposing his uncle from the throne.

Lesbos Island, once occupied by the French forces

Despite all the requests and promises made to him in Istanbul, the French ambassador left Istanbul without leaving even a charge d'affairs in his stead. Thus, the political relationship between the two states was severed.

The Ottoman Empire, however, did not want to pay the debt. Before long, the French added a three-point demand and cited the non-payment of debt as justification. They occupied the customs of Lesbos and informed that they would hold the proceeds to counter the debt. They refused to leave the island unless the assets of religious and cultural institutions of French nationality or those under their control were officially recognized.

The good feelings towards France felt by the Ottomans were shaken. In fact, the influence and dignity of France in the state was quite influential. The Public Debts administration, with its 700 civil servants, was almost entirely in the hands of France. The Ottoman Bank, which played an important role in the financial and economic life of the Ottoman Empire, was a British-French institution. The French investment capital in the Ottoman countries was over 2.5 billion francs. There were French institutions everywhere. French was taught in all the military and civil schools. Homeland freedom lovers always sought asylum in France and fought the autocratic administration from there. Furthermore, French officials also occupied the most important positions in state administration, finance, customs and public works.

Although the empire was hoping for help from Germany and Russia, against the French's unjust demands that were in violation of treaties, this was not coming. Eventually on 6 November 1901 the French demands had to be accepted. The French Navy withdrew from Lesbos.

REVOLUTION IN MACEDONIA

There were revolts and revolutions throughout the empire, and the tendencies towards dissolution and separation were accelerated. Even the declaration of the Reforms did not stop this situation. The Ottoman Empire had whetted the appetite of the Western states because of its wide geography. Every one of them was eager for its disintegration and getting the lion's share. In this period, the Ottoman State was called the 'Sick man of Europe' and this title passed into political terminology. Russia's Tsar Nicholas I was the first to use this expression.

Tsar Nicholas I of Russia (Yegor Botkin)

Macedonia occupied an important place within the European border. At that time the country had a population of 4 million, more than half of which was Muslim, while the rest was Christian. The majority of the Muslims were Turks and the rest were Albanians. Among the Christians, Macedonians were a majority, followed by Bulgarians, Greeks, Serbs, Vlachs (Romanians), Jews, Armenians, Bosnians, Gypsies and Croats.

Macedonia, which included the provinces of Thessaloniki, Manastir and Kosovo in the Ottoman administrative organization, was given to the Bulgarians by the Russians with the San Stefan treaty and handed back to the Ottoman Empire with the Berlin Treaty. Between these two treaties, the Bulgarians held Macedonia under their administration for just over four months. Based on this, they started to claim rights in the region. They set up revolutionary societies, formed gangs and supplied them with arms to this end.

The Bulgarians were against Turkish rule as well as other Christian minorities. They strictly wanted to dominate Macedonia by intimidating them. Therefore, they organized and armed the other Christian elements among themselves. Romania, Serbia and Greece were helping them. Sultan Abdulhamid, taking advantage of the competition among the Christians took care to keep them in balance. In this respect, the Bulgarians were careful not to oppress other Christians in their gang movements.

The Treaty of Berlin required reform in Macedonia as well as in Eastern Anatolia (Article 23). However, Sultan Abdulhamid did not allow the implementation of this article through his balance calculations. Before long the uprisings spiraled out of control. Although the Sublime Porte was in control of the case, the great powers that had signed the Berlin Treaty applied to the Sublime Porte and demanded the reform adopted for the Vilâyât-ı Selâse (three provinces), namely Thessaloniki, the Monastery and Kosovo, with Article 23 of this treaty to be put into force.

Sultan Abdulhamid appointed the governor of Yemen, Hüseyin Hilmi Pasha, as Inspector General for the three provinces mentioned. At the same time, a 'Rumelia provinces Reform Commission' was established in the Sublime Porte and Ferid Pasha, the Governor of Konya, was appointed as the chairman. Some of the articles prepared according to the instructions were as follows:

- Public and foreign affairs offices shall be established in every province,

- Governors shall work for the development of trade, agriculture and industry,

- The Gendarmerie and the police shall include both Muslims and Christians,

- The local military units shall be at the disposal of the governor,

- Military courts with both Muslim and Christian representation shall be established in each town.

In spite of the German measures, Austria and Russia did not see the

A political cartoon showing the representatives of many of the nations involved in the Treaty of Berlin

reform program as adequate, and on 21 February 1903 they presented a new program titled the 'Vienna Reform Program '.

Although the Ottoman Empire accepted this program, Bulgaria found it not adequate, again. Soon the revolution of 2 August 1903 broke out in Macedonia. The Ottoman Bank in Thessaloniki was blown up with dynamite. During the St. Elias celebration, the intimidation and terror movements of the gangs started. Thirty-thousand gang members were involved in the massacre and plunder against all elements in Macedonia. Greek gangs and Serbian gangs came to the aid of their compatriots. Meanwhile, Albania was discussing the idea of an autonomous or independent Albania. They even killed the Serb consul in Mitrovica. Balkans continued to seethe internally.

A MESSAGE TO THE ALBANIANS

The events in Bulgaria, Greece and Macedonia brought up the issue of the autonomy of Albania from time to time and various movements occurred. On the chaos that left the Ottoman administration in a difficult position, Sultan Abdulhamid addressed the Albanians as follows:

"Oh people of Albania, who are superior and famous for their sense of honor, intention, courage and strength. (...)

"Albania's districts have been governed by a single province, and now there are rumors that the Albanians want to establish a new form of government titled 'Tevhid-i İdare'.

"Rulers are inspired by God. Our hearts are not satisfied that the people of Albania unite in such a desire (...)

"The meaning of this kind of administration is broad, but it is the extract of this meaning and its consequences, for example, to separate the provinces of Manastır, Kosovo, Ioannina and Shkodra provinces together

Ali Pasha of Tepedelen

with the banners attached to them, and establish a sick administration that is contrary to the Sharia procedures and regulations valid in other Ottoman States?

"Do you know what kind of unhealthy thought process those five-ten hellraisers of this illegitimate attempt is based on?

"Since Albania is surrounded by Austria and Greece on land as well as surrounded by Italy from the sea, those five-ten hellraisers whose names will be cursed from here to doomsday due to nature and intentions will be instigated by foreigners and promises of illegal interests, encouragement and goading — as is their nature — will not be able to resist and these fools intend to separate these provinces from the empire by manifesting various deceptive occasions and reasons, and after a short period of time, they intend to assimilate our procedures and customs and natures with governments that do not comply with our nature.

'Overwhelmed by the deceased commander Ali Pasha of Tepedelen's independent and excessive ways, the peril that occurred within a short period of time the Muslim of Euboea (Eğriboz), Mora and their vicinity passed into the hands of the Turks of Greek origin and formed the State of Greece.

"Was it not the Tevhid-i İdare (Administrative Unity) idea that is a vicious thought that separated Crimea from the Ottoman Empire and the people of Dagestan from their state and made them ready to be plucked by foreigners.

"The malevolent thoughts of the of these greedy and illegitimate mischief makers are in the direction of various illegitimate and illogical idiots plotting to separate these places from the Ottoman administration for deceptive reasons and interests, and carries out the betrayal of the religion, state and homeland for their personal interests.

'If such plots and deceptions are not taken into account, the ideas of these hellraisers remain unrealized. If sheep under the protection and care of a shepherd stray from the flock of course they will become feed for wolves.

'A parable comes to mind; it is possible to put two wet or dry wands together and break them with a movement. However, it is not possible to break up to 20-30 wands in one move, is not it?

"How can the Ottoman State facilitate and support losing these provinces that have been conquered with bloodshed and unbearable challenges to foreigners?"[2]

2 My Views of the State and the Country 1, A.Atilla Çetin, p.14-15, Çamlıca Printing House, Istanbul, June 2011.

Sultan Murad V, the 33th Sultan of the Ottoman Empire

THE DEMISE OF MURAD V

While the Sultan was grappling with the issues of the state, the news of the death of his uncle's son, the former ruler Murad V was delivered. Murad V, who passed away at the age of 64 on 29 August 1904 had been living with his family in Çırağan Palace for 28 years after he was deposed. During this time, he never left the palace. Sultan Abdulhamid Han had taken care of him personally and sent famous doctors of the day to cure him, and he recovered after a while. Abdulhamid Han asked after him from time to time by sending a statesman.

The death of Sultan Murad was caused by diabetes. He had spent his days in Ciragan Palace occupied with the education of his grandchildren and music.

Sultan Abdulhamid organized the funeral of Murad V and had him buried in the tomb of Yeni Mosque, where his mother Şevkefza Valide Sultan was buried.

Edward Jorris, leader of the assassination team that attempted to murder the Caliph

ASSASSINATION ATTEMPT AGAINST ABDULHAMİD II

On Friday, July 21, 1905, a time bomb was exploded among hundreds of people who came to watch the salutation ceremony as Sultan Abdulhamid was about to leave Yildiz Mosque. The target of this bomb was actually Abdulhamid II. However, the planning was off.

The Armenian committees who lived as a minority and dispersed throughout six provinces in East Anatolia who were living the reverie of establishing an independent Armenia had resorted to the eradication of the Sultan as a last resort. First, a carefully set time bomb would be detonated when the Sultan left Friday prayer, and then bombs would be detonated at foreign embassies, Tunnel, Galata Bridge, the Sublime Porte and the Ottoman Bank to generate chaos. By generating chaos in Istanbul the actual and military intervention of Europe would be ensured. Subsequently they were planning to seize the provinces in East Anatolia. All preparations had been made.

The assassins were three Russian Armenians, namely Samoil Kayın a.k.a. Hristofor Mikaelyan of the Armenian Revolution Society from Baku, his daughter Robina Kayın and Konstantin Kabulyan a.k.a. Safo. They made plans for a month in Beyoğlu in Moravic apartment building and prepared their crew in Istanbul. They had engaged an international hitman named Charles Edouard Jorris from Antwerp, one of the Belgian anarchists in particular. This 29-year-old young anarchist who had been in Istanbul for four years, is considered to be the soul and the most important operative and perpetrator in the 'Bomb Incident'.

The ringleaders from abroad went to observe the Sultan's salutation ceremony and determined that it took the sultan a full minute and forty-two seconds to get from Hamidiye Mosque in Yıldız to the outer door and returned to Europe to return two months later. During this time, the elegant car was built in Vienna according to a special plan to accommodate the bomb. The vehicle was disassembled into pieces to be re-assembled in Istanbul. A bomb consisting of eighty kilograms of 'Mélinite' and "Twenty pounds of Mitraille = a bomb made of steel and iron shrapnel' was placed into a 100 kg volume chest into this rubber wheeled car.

"How can the Ottoman State facilitate and support losing these provinces that have been conquered with bloodshed and unbearable challenges to foreigners?"[3]

THE DEMISE of MURAD V

While the Sultan was grappling with the issues of the state, the news of the death of his uncle's son, the former ruler Murad V was delivered. Murad V, who passed away at the age of 64 on 29 August 1904 had been living with his family in Çırağan Palace for 28 years after he was deposed. During this time, he never left the palace. Sultan Abdulhamid Han had taken care of him personally and sent famous doctors of the day to cure him, and he recovered after a while. Abdulhamid Han asked after him from time to time by sending a statesman.

The death of Sultan Murad was caused by diabetes. He had spent his days in Ciragan Palace occupied with the education of his grandchildren and music.

Sultan Abdulhamid organized the funeral of Murad V and had him buried in the tomb of Yeni Mosque, where his mother Şevkefza Valide Sultan was buried.

3 My Views of the State and the Country 1, A.Atilla Çetin, p.14-15, Çamlıca Printing House, Istanbul, June 2011.

The Ciragan Palaca on the shore of the Strait

ASSASSINATION ATTEMPT AGAINST ABDULHAMİD II

On Friday, July 21, 1905, a time bomb was exploded among hundreds of people who came to watch the salutation ceremony as Sultan Abdulhamid was about to leave Yildiz Mosque. The target of this bomb was actually Abdulhamid II. However, the planning was off.

The Armenian committees who lived as a minority and dispersed throughout six provinces in East Anatolia who were living the reverie of establishing an independent Armenia had resorted to the eradication of the Sultan as a last resort. First, a carefully set time bomb would be detonated when the Sultan left Friday prayer, and then bombs would be detonated at foreign embassies, Tunnel, Galata Bridge, the Sublime Porte and the Ottoman Bank to generate chaos. By generating chaos in Istanbul the actual and military intervention of Europe would be ensured. Subsequently they were planning to seize the provinces in East Anatolia. All preparations had been made.

The assassins were three Russian Armenians, namely Samoil Kayın a.k.a. Hristofor Mikaelyan of the Armenian Revolution Society from Baku, his daughter Robina Kayın and Konstantin Kabulyan a.k.a. Safo. They made plans for a month in Beyoğlu in Moravic apartment building and prepared their crew in Istanbul. They had engaged an international hitman named Charles Edouard Jorris from Antwerp, one of the Belgian anarchists in particular. This 29-year-old young anarchist who had been in Istanbul for four years, is considered to be the soul and the most important operative and perpetrator in the 'Bomb Incident'.

The Selamlik at the Hamidiye Mosque on Friday (Abdullah Frères)

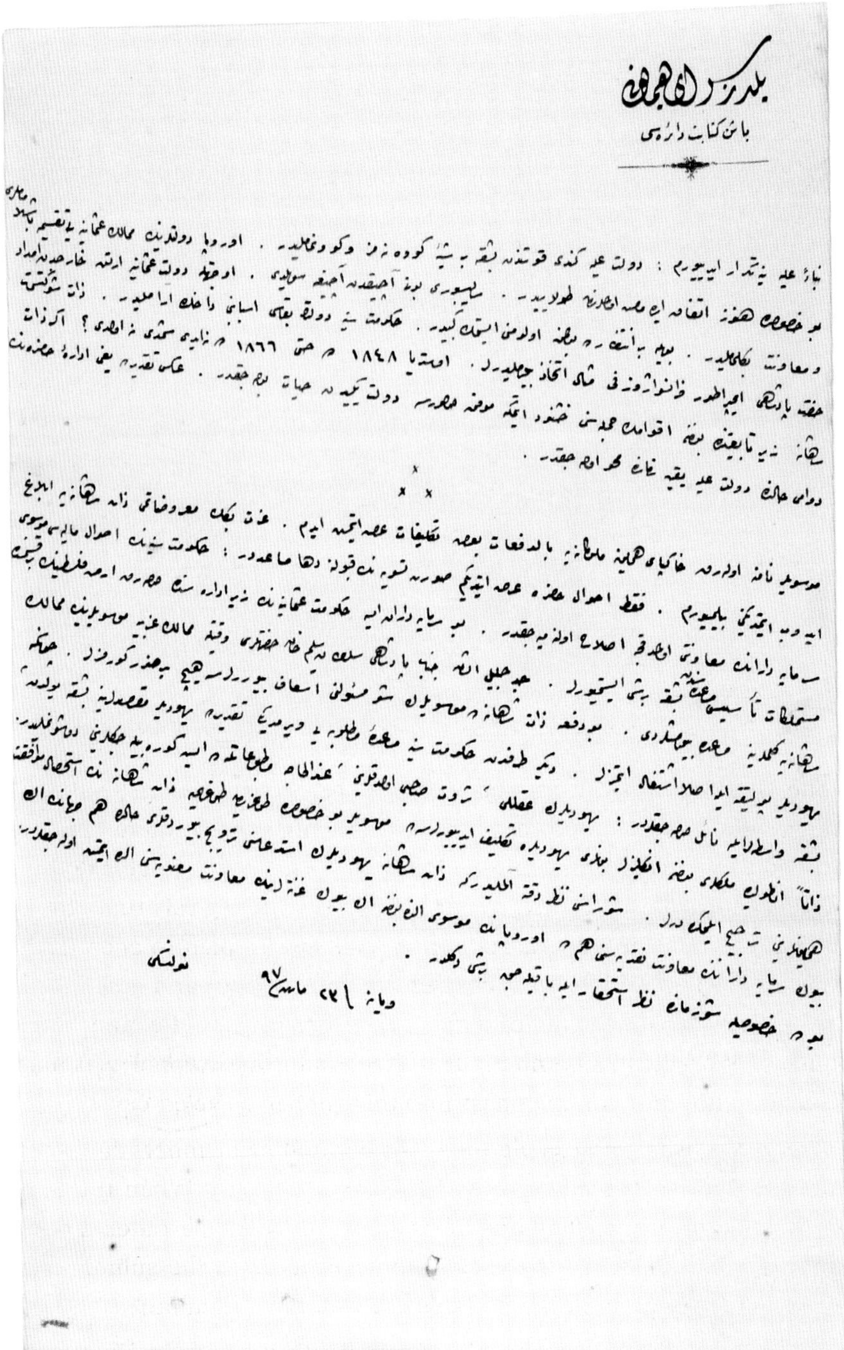
یلدز سرای همایونی
باش کتابت دائره سی

Sultan had also to care about the menaces made by the Zionists in order for getting some land in Palestine. A letter by Philipp Michael Newlinski, the diplomatic agent of Zionist leader Theodor Herzl, menacing the Sultan

The specially-manufactured carriage used for the assassination trial

The ringleaders from abroad went to observe the Sultan's salutation ceremony and determined that it took the sultan a full minute and forty-two seconds to get from Hamidiye Mosque in Yıldız to the outer door and returned to Europe to return two months later. During this time, the elegant car was built in Vienna according to a special plan to accommodate the bomb. The vehicle was disassembled into pieces and assembled in Istanbul. A bomb consisting of eighty kilograms of 'Mélinite' and "Twenty pounds of Mitraille = a bomb made of steel and iron shrapnel' was placed into a 100 kilogram volume chest into this rubber wheeled car.

Everything was going as planned. The committee members came to the salutation ceremony in the guise of European tourists. When the Sultan was in Yıldız Mosque, they abandoned the car near the outer gate and retreated. The bomb inside the car would explode as the sultan walked between the mosque and the sultan's car and kill the sultan.

Sultan Hamid had talked with Şeyhülislâm Cemâlüddin Efendi more than usual and complimenting the ministers and viziers saluting him in the corridor as was leaving the mosque after the prayer. That is why he was a little late for the bomb clock that had been set. Therefore, the assassins' calculations went belly up and when the sultan walked from the

A panorama of Istanbul showing the Kadıköy shores and the islands of Marmara

hallway to the outer door, the so-called 'hell-machine' exploded with a great noise in accordance with the planned time. The sound of the explosion was heard in all parts of Istanbul, even from Üsküdar, Kadıköy, Göztepe and Erenköy vicinity.

The Armenian committee members had not reached their goals. However, at the end of this explosion, 26 people were killed, 58 were injured comprised of officers, drivers, soldiers and people. Everybody was fleeing, no one knew what was happening. The Sultan did not panic, he stood at the top of the stairs and watched calmly. The Sultan got into his car with a few brief orders and went to Yıldız Palace, where he met foreign envoys and statesmen without disrupting his usual schedule.

On the following day, an investigation commission was established under the presidency of Necib Melhame Pasha, the undersecretary of the Ministry of Commerce and Public Works. The assassins escaped using their foreign passports. Only the Belgian anarchist was caught and confessed in detail to his actions in the presence of the Belgian ambassador. Even though the anarchist was condemned to death Sultan Abdulhamid pardoned him. Jorris was brought from his prison cell to the palace to meet the Sultan. Jorris who was tasked with assassinating Sultan Hamid entered his service in exchange for money to work against the Armenian committees and to gather intelligence. He was five hundred gold coins as per diem and put on a train in Sirkedji station and went. Jorris who was tasked with assassinating Sultan Abdulhamid returned to Europe as the sultan's agent who would serve for a long time.

In the meantime, many Armenians were arrested in connection with the assassination attempt. Many bombs and various explosives were re-

The Sirkedji Railway Station

covered. However, Ablulhamid Han chose not to act violently in this incident targeting his own person and in fact preferred to forget it.

One of the most grievous aspects of the 'Bomb Incident' organized by the Russian-Armenian Committee members was the fact that various Turkish intellectuals opposing Sultan Abdulhamid applauded the incident. For example, Tevfik Fikret says in his poetry" "Bir lâhza-i teahhur" recites the following :

Ey şanlı avcı, dâmını bîhûde kurmadın,

Attın fakat yazık ki, yazıklar ki vurmadın!

(O glorious hunter, you didn't set your trap in vain / It is a pity you missed)

Likewise, author and historian Ahmed Refiq reveals the outlook of his country regarding the sultan as follows:

"Finally, the truth was completely revealed: it is understood that this heroic movement was executed by our Armenian citizens in order to free the Ottoman nation from the persecution of Abdulhamid."

The failure of the bomb attempt was met with disillusionment by the Greeks, Jews and Armenians, as well as by the enemies of the unwary sultan. The Greek minority was angry with the sultan who had defeated Greece, and the Armenians were already known to have an axe to grind. The Jews were unable to get over the immediate rejection of the proposal by the sultan when the Zionists had offered to purchase Palestine for millions in gold a few years back.

There were other assassinations around the world at that time. At the beginning of 1878, assassinations were carried out against the German

The famous Turkish historian Ahmed Refiq

emperor and the king of Italy. The king and queen of Spain did not survive the assassination against them (1879). They were followed by the assassination of the Russian Emperor Alexander II (1881) and the Serbian king (1882). The assassination attempt on the queen of England coincided in the same year (1882). The King of Romania was attacked in 1888, Prince Ferdinand was attacked in 1890 and the Austrian emperor was attacked in 1891 with explosives. The crown prince of Russia was the victim of the same terror. It is interesting that Sultan Abdulhamid lived a long life in era of these attacks and assassinations and died in his bed.

Sultan Abdulhamid II

HAMİDİYE-HEJAZ RAILROAD

The railway that Sultan Abdulhamid II was planning to construct on Ottoman territory was primarily considered as a military, strategic and political necessity. His experiences revealed how accurate his opinion was. For example, during the campaign of 93, he saw the benefits of the Istanbul-Plovdiv railway in the deployment of troops while he had been aware of the problems caused by the lack of a railway during the Bosnia Herzegovina revolution and the Serbia and Montenegro wars. In this context, the military facilitation provided by the Thessaloniki-Istanbul and Manastir-Thessaloniki lines in the 1897 Ottoman-Greek war, which he had ordered to build, inspired the sultan to accelerate the railroad building. The sultan was also aware of the economic and political benefits that the railroads would bring.

Abdulhamid Han II was able to increase the total of 1,783 kilometers of the Ottoman railway line which used to be 1145 before 1878 to 1,193 in Rumelia and to 2,500 kilometers in Anatolia to total 3,700 kilometers.

The railway would be one of the pillars that would maintain the state politically and economically. In his memoirs, he describes this project as 'Through the Baghdad railway, the existing European-Indian trade route will be useful again. If this road unites Syria and Beirut to establish contacts with Alexandria and Haifa, a new trade route will have emerged. This path will not only provide economic benefits for our state, but it will also be very important in terms of military maintenance as it will also reinforce our strength in these areas.'

The main railroad station at the Western gate, Medina

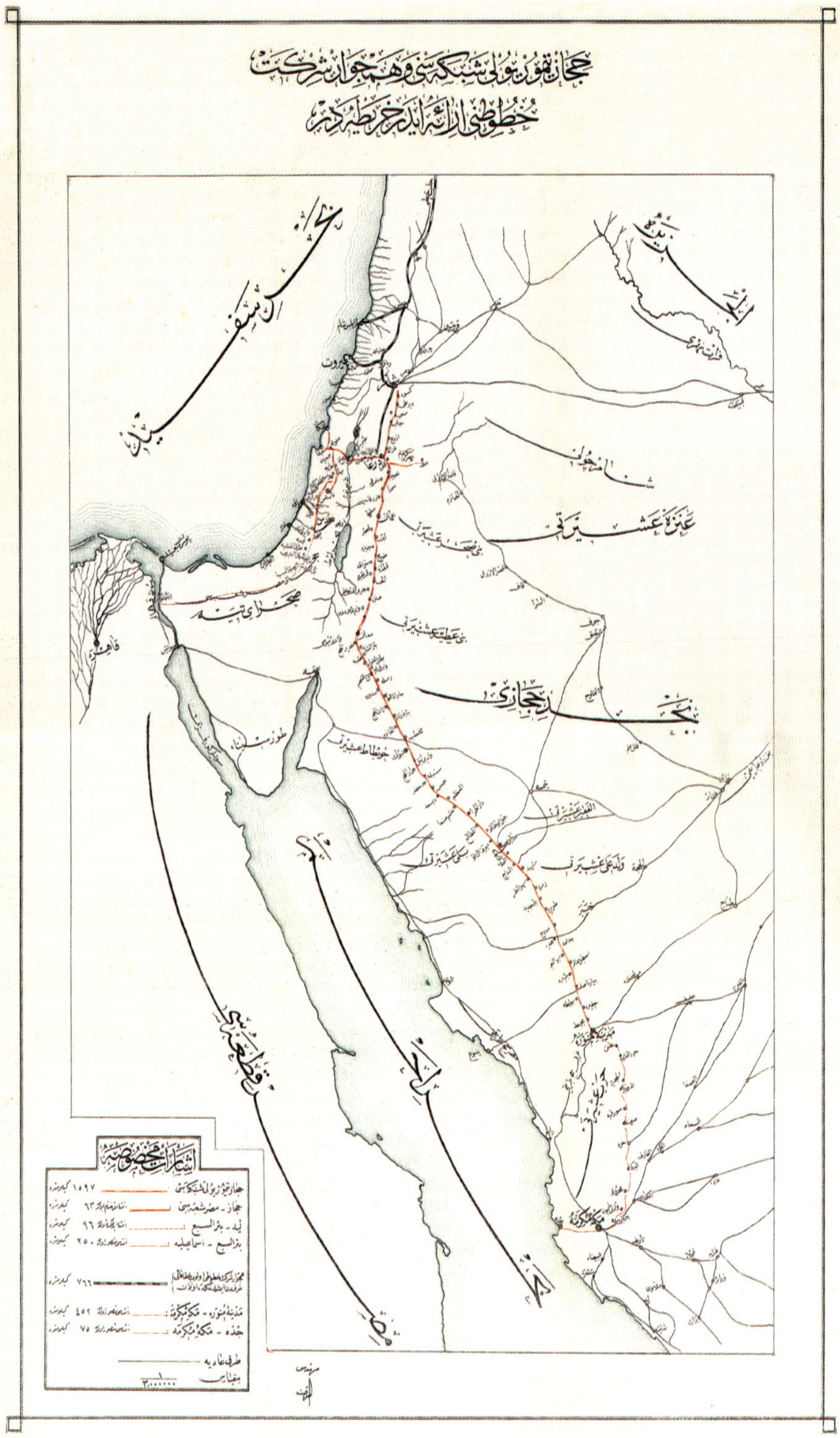

The Hejaz Railway map

Hejaz occupied a special place and importance for Sultan Abdulhamid Han II. Due to the presence of the sacred cities of Muslims, Mecca Al-Mukarrama and Medina al-Munawwara, and the sultan being the Caliph, he was closely involved with the whole Arabian Peninsula and Hejaz in particular. The sultan of Hejaz. Arabia had become a new target and area of interest for European imperialism. The only thing to be done under these circumstances was to protect this vast territory, including the Muslim qibla, against external and internal dangers at any cost.

Sultan Abdulhamid II had all the proposals related to the laying of the railway studied by experts and collected their opinions on the subject.

Several proposals for the Hejaz Railway had been made until that time. The first serious project was made in 1864 by German-American Engineer Dr. Carl-Friedrich Zimpel. In 1872, Wilhelm von Pressel prepared a railway project for the Ottomans. In 1874, when Ahmed Reşid joined the campaign in Yemen, he realized that there was a need for a railway to transport troops and presented a railway project from Damascus to Mecca and from there to Jeddah. Similarly, by 1880, Minister for Public Works Hasan Fehmi Pasha presented a project which started in Izmir and ended in Baghdad by passing through Eskisehir, Konya, Aleppo and Anbar. The Hejaz line he proposed moved from Aleppo to Orunt Valley in Hama and from there to Hummus, continued to Damascus and from there to Havran Sahara and Yordan Valley and reached Bahr-i Lut and finally Hejaz from there. Project proposals were likewise made by Osman Nuri Pasha in 1884, District Governor Doctor Şakir in 1890, Süleyman Şefik and Jeddah Director of Ewqaf in 1892, Muhammed İnşâallah Efendi in 1897.

Conflicts of interest of the great states were also raised on the agenda of rail concessions. British ambassador Henry Layard asserted that if the British built the railway that would connect Istanbul to Baghdad and Basra, all safety would be provided by the British, so that Ottoman territory would be protected against Russian expansionism. The Sultan gave the French the construction of the railways in Syria and Palestine. The Jaffa-Jerusalem line was commissioned in 1891, the Müzeyrib (Havran) line in 1894 and the Beirut-Damascus line in 1895.

The Baghdad Railway concession was given to the Germans. Thus, the sultan was initiating the Hejaz Railway project, which he had been planning for a long time. This railway, which was planned to be connected to the Baghdad line, would be extended from Istanbul to Damascus and from there to Medina-i Al-Munawwara, then to Mecca al-Mukarrama and Jeddah, and finally to Baghdad and Basra via Yemen and Central Arabia.

The Dead Sea, its shores bordering Jordan

With the execution of the Hejaz Railroad, the pilgrimage obligation which took months between Damascus-Mecca would be reduced to 18 days. If the railway was connected to Jeddah, it would be easy to reach all over the world by sea.

The Sultan initiated the preparations for the Hejaz Railway with his order on May 2, 1900. The railway line was to be built along the historic pilgrimage route. Construction began with an official ceremony in Kadem district of Damascus on September 1, 1900, the 25th anniversary of the sultan's accession to the throne.

The total cost of the railway which would initially extend to Mecca al-Mukarrama was estimated to be 4 million TL. This was a huge figure for the Ottoman finance. In fact, this figure corresponded to 18% of the total expenditure of Ottoman finance in 1901. It was not possible to allocate an extra allowance from the budget because a large part of the government revenues were planned for expenditures.

Expenditures such as the payment of foreign debts and installments of war reparations were dragging the state's financial situation into

One of the dozens of clock towers built for the 25th anniversary of the Sultan's accession to the throne, Jaffa

bankruptcy. How would the state that could not balance its budget because of financial instability every year or even pay the salaries of civil servants regularly hope to realize this project? In fact, this project would not only be the project of the Ottoman State, but the project of all Muslims. With this thought, the sultan launched a donation campaign with a personal donation of 50 thousand liras, and the construction continued with the help of many statesmen and the public.

In addition to the Ottoman geography, help came from Muslims in places such as Central Asia, Africa, Europe, America, India, Russia, Pakistan. These donations were the most important financial source of the project. In addition, mandatory deductions were made from civil servant salaries, official papers and documents were sold for the benefit of the railroad, stamps and postcards were issued, revenues from the hides of sacrificed animals were transferred here, even the operation concessions of some mines were transferred.

In those days while 150 kilometers of railway could be constructed per year, the Hejaz Railway line managed to lay 288 kilometers in a year despite desert temperatures and material impossibilities.

Initially, on September 1, 1901, the Müzeyrib-Der'a (11 kilometers) line was opened. Der'a-Zerka (79 kilometers) was completed on 1 September 1902, Zerka-Amman (20 kilometers) on 19 November 1902, Damascus-Der'a on September 1, 1903 and Damascus-Ma'an on September

1, 1904 (460 kilometers). Until 1906, 750 kilometers of the Hejaz Railway line was laid. On September 1, 1906, 233 km of Ma'an-Tebük line and in 1907 the 288-kilometer Tebük-El-Ulâ line was opened. The 323-km Al-Ulâ-Medina al-Munawwara line was opened with a big ceremony on September 1, 1908 in the 33rd year of the reign of Sultan Abdulhamid II. In September 1908, the Hejaz Railway reached 1,464 kilometers. Thus, the Damascus-Medina al-Munawwara route that 40 days with caravans was reduced to three days with trains.

During construction many stations, bridges, tunnels, ponds, factories and various buildings were built. The cost of the completed lines was 3 million 66 thousand 167 lira. In this case, it was a more affordable cost than railway construction by European companies.

The planned Medina-i Al-Munawwara-Mecca al-Mukarrama, Mecca al-Mukarrama-Jeddah and Yemen lines could not be realized. What is more, after the Second Constitutional Monarchy, the Committee of Union and Progress, which took over the administration, would remove a large number of experienced high-ranking civil servants from the railway line. They would be replaced by officers who had been dismissed from Yıldız Palace, the sailors and dispatchers who had been working in Haifa for years would be dismissed. In the next period, many civil servants would resign because of attacks and impossible working conditions and it would be necessary to resort to newspaper advertisements to engage officers to work here.

The west gate of Jiddah, Saudi Arabia

THE SULTAN'S AQABA MOVE

Parallel to the various events taking place in Anatolia and Rumelia, important developments were also taking place in the Arabian territory of the state.

After Yavuz Sultan Selim's conquest of Egypt he received the title of Caliph and for 389 years until the Aqaba depression the Ottoman sultans had given utmost importance to using this title. They had done their traditional duties regarding Haremeyn as the Caliphate and considered themselves the leaders of the Islamic world.

Separating the great peninsula that was host to the origin of Islam, the homeland of Arabis and being a permanent visiting place of the whole Islam realm as a result of Mecca al-Mukarrama and Medina-i Al-Munawwara from Ottoman domination or at least causing the Arab world to rise against that domination would be a most effective blow against an Ottoman Leader. Therefore, during the reign of Sultan Abdulhamid II, Jaziratu'l-Arab became the most important stage of the Turkish-British political struggle.

The most vital points of this historical struggle on both sides of the peninsula are as follows:

One is the port of Kuwait to the south of the Gulf of Basra and one Kal'at'ül-Akabe or Kasr al-Aqaba, which is on the upper border of the Gulf of Aqaba in the southeast of the Red Sea and four kilometers east of the coast. The first of these two points was at the end of the Bağdad railway and therefore the most important port of trade in Anatolia and Iraq, and the second one meant the gate of the Hejaz line into the Red Sea through the Gulf of Aqaba. In the case of the former, the Turkish-British struggle took place by directing and supporting local sheikhs and in the latter direct military action took place. Sultan Hamid, who also benefited from German politics regarding the Kuwait issue due to the Baghdad railway, was alone against England on the Aqaba issue.

The Haydarpaşa-Baghdad line, which led the Germans to "Drang nach Ostn" in other words the 'move to the east' policy to the Gulf of Basra over Kuwait, and consequently down to the Indian road, would be a way to take its power into the Jazirat-ül-Arab through the influence of the Caliphate. At the end of this road, the quay of Kuwait was under Ottoman rule. After a while some of the sheikhs in the area came under the influence of the British, the sultan held various negotiations, some land battles ensued.

Selim the Grim or the conqueror of Egypt

Haydarpasha Railroad Station, Istanbul

The power struggle here which had festered since 1897 and intensified with the instigation of the British into a bloody feud in 1904 with the continuing Yemeni rebellion. Although British politics ended the influence of the Caliphate in the Kuveyt-Hayl-Rıyâd struggle center and east of the Arabian Peninsula, it was not so successful in northwestern Yemen.

While the Macedonian issue threatened the Ottoman domination in Rumelia because of joint interventions and threats of the European states, the future of Arabia and even Iraq and ElJazira was jeopardized with the entry of British influence in the eastern part of Jazirat'ül-Arab and Sultan Hamid prioritized winning in the west of this peninsula what he had lost in the east.

Although he had always been wary towards the great states, he resisted and even fought in the end alone against this issue against both British imperialism and the other great states that supported it. The aim of this struggle was to seize the Aqaba fortress, which was the most important gateway to the Red Sea by the Hejaz railway as well as the main line of the Caliphate policy in the east, against Kuwait, the last point of the Baghdad line. This vital point on Ottoman territory had been in the hands of the Egyptian guard with the permission of the Sublime Porte since the settlement in the Egypt issue during the era of Mehmed Ali Pasha. The reason for this was the passage of the highway from Egypt to Hajj

Actually, since the province of Egypt was dominated by the Ottomans, it would be normal to grant such a permission in terms of the security of the pilgrimage road. In fact, a number of Egyptian outposts had been built in some places along the Hejaz terrain. However, after the opening of the Suez canal, Egyptian pilgrims abandoned land transport and preferred the sea route while the British occupation of 1882 had transformed this Egyptian province into a British base of action. So much so that Britain had ideas of taking the Hejaz railway, Palestine and Syria under control by reinforcing this military point.

The Sultan was aware of this sensitive situation in the region. Sultan Hamid's basis for the occupation of the Aqaba castle when Hamidiye Hejaz Railway approached the Gulf of Aqaba was to save the point of contact with the sea against the British threat.

The most severe phase of the political crisis called the 'Aqaba issue' began Britain's ten-day ultimatum: Ottoman forces were required to evacuate the Sinai peninsula during this time. For this threat, navy was deployed from Malta, a British fleet set off in the Aegean Sea and even the Ocean Navy showed itself in Gibraltar.

Sultan Hamid's intention was not to declare war on Britain. The Sublime Porte responded positively to the British ultimatum however since Sultan Hamid did not regard Britain's occupation of Egypt as legitimate, he wanted only Turkish and Egyptian officers on the commission that was going to determine the new border, so he had not allowed British officers to be present.

The negotiations of the Commission resulted in the signing of an eight-point protocol: the border line identified in this contract started on the west coast of the Gulf of Aqaba, from the Re sahils-Tâbe and overlooked the Mediterranean coast and descended to the water front from the top of the Harâbe between Gaza and Al-Arish.

Thus, the main target of Sultan Abdulhamid II, the Aqaba remained with the Ottomans and only Tabe at the Egyptian border was returned. British imperialism, which wanted to strangle the Arabian peninsula with the Kuveyt-Aqaba-San tongs succeeded only in Kuwait, while Caliphate policies prevailed in the other two points.

THE FIRST STEP TO THE WORLD WAR: REVAL MEETING

The Ottoman Empire lost its dominance in North African countries in the last half century, and in 25 and thirty years it had lost its leadership in places such as Serbia, Montenegro, Romania, Bulgaria, Crete and Cyprus. There were bloody riots in the remaining lands of Macedonia, Eastern

18419. P. Z.

Biblioteca e Caffé della Regina, Malta

Nicholas II looking down a massive army, and behind him 'Peace' seems concerned (Udo J. Keppler)

Anatolia and the Arabian Peninsula. Public Debts Administration exploited the financial resources of the state, privileged foreign partners were consuming the economic power. Revenue sources were either in the hands of foreigners or minorities who were foreign fans.

The world states, aware of this difficult situation of the Ottoman Empire, were also aware that the world was on the verge of a great war. In such an environment, the meeting of King of England, Edward the Seventh, and the Russian Tsar Nicholas II in Reval, Estonia, was the first step of the great war. The aim of this meeting on June 9, 1908 was to take measures against the German threat, which was increasingly strong and would lead Europe to a great war. Apparently only the reform of Macedonia was thought to be under discussion.

The approach of the Russians to the British had brought Austria closer to Germany, and Italy saw its own interests necessitated merging with this bloc. This manifested a triple alliance. The Kayser hoped that including the Ottoman State in this alliance would bring great advantages. Sultan Hamid, on the other hand, was cautious because of his policy not to be instrumental to any state's ambition.

On the other hand, France decided to stand by the UK. This would also promulgate a tripartite alliance. It was certain that these two forces would

Flags of World War I allies (M. Pozzi)

soon collide and one would ruin the other. Abdulhamid Han was aware of this and therefore he intended to get rid of all capitulations and all foreign pressures and interventions on condition that he could remain neutral. Sultan Hamid who acted with great sensitivity in terms of this meeting and the Emperor of Germany Wilhelm II communicated immediately and it was decided that the emperor would come to Istanbul to meet with Sultan Hamid.

On the other hand, the decisions of the Reval meeting triggered another movement in the Ottoman State. The Committee of Union and Progress which was against Sultan Abdulhamid II and especially the regime, had taken action by claiming that the settlement of the Ottoman geography had been agreed upon during the Reval meeting.

OPPOSITION AGAINST THE SULTAN

THE FIRST MOTION AGAINST THE SULTAN: YOUNG TURKS

During the 33 years that he was on the throne Sultan Abdulhamid Khan, who had been acting for the interests of the state and the nation and even implemented prohibitions when necessary, had to deal not only with foreign countries but also with internal opposition. During the reign of Abdulhamid, the libertarian and nationalist currents in the world were increasing, and the Ottoman absolutistic administration was receiving severe criticism.

When the sultan succeeded to the throne, he declared the constitutional monarchy administration, but it didn't take long for him to realize that this administration was leading the state to disintegration. Over time, he administered single handedly and failed to re-implement the constitutional administration. What was essential for him was to be able to preserve the weakened state which had received severe blows without great losses. However, it was not enough for the new generations that were supported and even trained by foreign outlets. In the course of time young officers and intellectuals who found support with the public and admired Europe moved away from the realities of their homeland and remained alien to the history of the state and tradition that kept the state standing. The cost of their enthusiasm would be high for the whole world...

The revision of the Ottoman Empire according to the requirements of the century begins in the period of Sultan Mahmud II and continued with the Reform that was declared with the Imperial Edict of Gulhane in 1839 in the period of Sultan Abdulmecid. The modernization and renewal period, which began with the Reform period, manifested in the form of Westernization, spreading in the upper layer which could be called the bourgeois. Furthermore, in the last century the Ottoman State began to

Sultan Abdulhamid in his later days of reign, going to or turning back from a procession

be inadequate in the dominance of the vast geography and the statesmen's lack of merit, disloyalty and even betrayal resulted in the inability to counter the needs of different nations. It was up to Sultan Abdulhamid II, who had succeeded to the throne during the ongoing decline and weakening period, to make the necessary investments in political, economic, social and technical terms to prevent the collapse of the state.

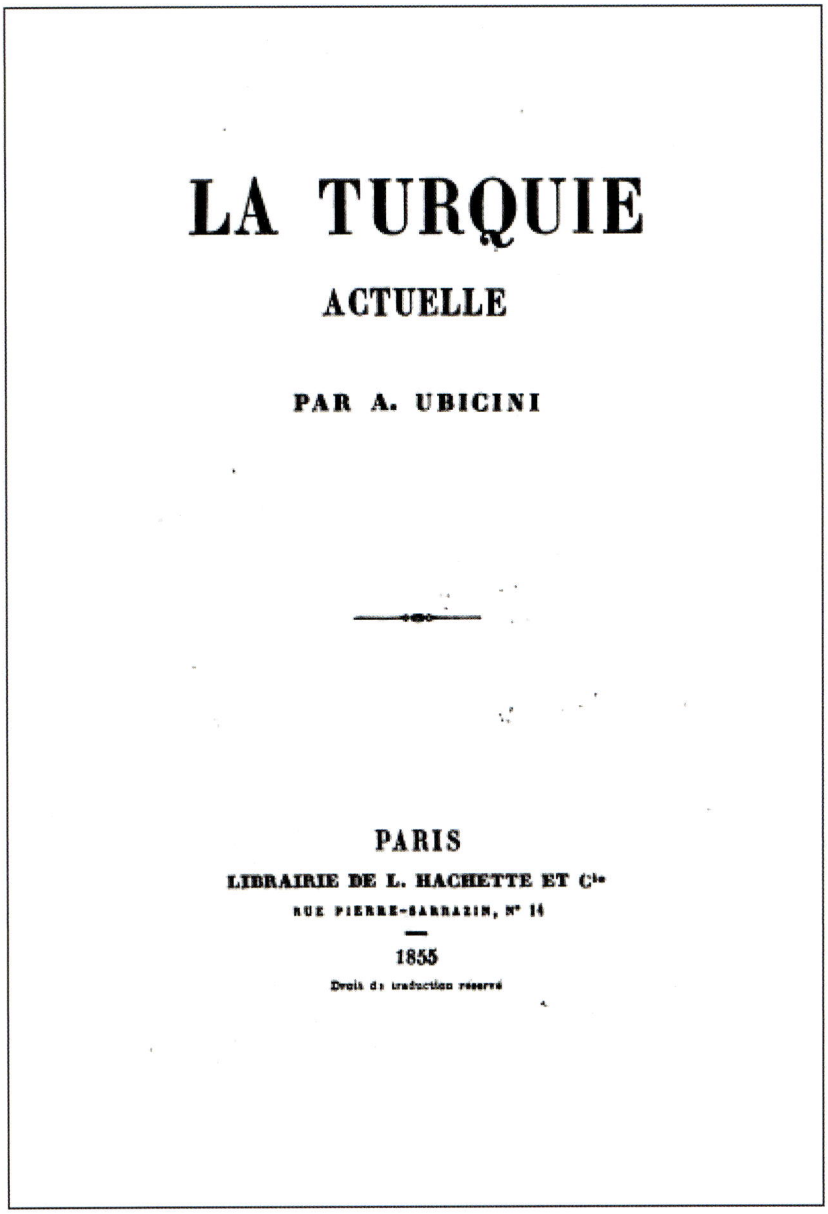
LA TURQUIE

ACTUELLE

PAR A. UBICINI

PARIS

LIBRAIRIE DE L. HACHETTE ET Cie

RUE PIERRE-SARRAZIN, N° 14

1855

Droit de traduction réservé

The title page of Ubicini's famous work on Turkey

The first serious movement of dissident power, that gathered plenty of supporters in the period of Abdulhamid Han, was the Young Turk / Young (New) Ottoman movement. This term was first introduced into literature by Abdolonyme Ubicini in 1855, both in terms of statesmen who participated in the reform movement during the Mahmud II period, and in the words of Jeune Turquie de Mahmoud and Jeune Turquie d'Abdul Medjid to describe the pro-Western Reform supporters during the era of Sultan Abdulmecid. It was used by Mustafa Fâzıl Pasha himself and the European press in order to identify the New Ottomans who organized an opposition movement in Europe with the financial support of the Pasha in the 1860s. Mustafa Fâzıl Pasha, in his letter to the Sultan Abdulaziz, dated 7 February 1867, wrote 'great party of the young Turks' and described 'jeune Turquie' as an opposition organization to 'old Turk' in the founding document of the Young Ottomans Society. In addition to this, the concept began to appear in literature for the reintroduction of the Constitutional Law immediately after the recess of the Ottoman Parliament and for the people who advocated the constitutional administration. With such a comprehensive and ambiguous use, almost all opponents of Abdulhamid's administration had been identified as Young Turks. On the other hand, the fact that the concept was used for a group instead of certain individuals, disturbed Abdulhamid II and, in 1901, he ruled that the 'hellraiser' was to replace 'Young Turk'. After this date the terminology used in official documents instead of this concept was 'plotters'.

Mustafa Fazıl Pasha, the Egyptian notable who had an open supoort for the revolutionary-minded Turks

The Teşebbüs-i Şahsî ve Adem-i Merkeziyet Society founded by Prince Sabahaddin Bey and his supporters, organized the Young Turks as an intellectual movement within the framework of Western ideas while trying to transform the Eastern Anatolian uprisings into a general revolution along with the Dashnaksutyun Society.

The following names can be mentioned as foremost Young Turks: Abdullah Cevdet, Abdurrahman Bedirhan, Ahmed Rızâ, Ahmed Fazlı (Tung), Ahmed Ferid (Tek), Ahmed Kemal (Akünal), Ahmed Lutfullah, Ahmed Niyazi, Ahmed Sâib, Ali Fahri, Ali Fehmi, Ali Haydar Midhat, Ali Şefkatî, Bahâeddin Şâkir, Derviş Hima (Maksud Ibrahim Naxhi Spahiu), Edhem Ruhi (Balkan), Emîr Şekîb Arslan, Halil Ganem, Hüseyin Tosun, Hüsrev Sami (Kızıldoğan), Hüseyinzâde Ali (Turan), İbrâhim Temo, İshak Sükûtî, İsmail Canbolat, İsmâil Enver Bey (Pasha), İsmâil Kemal, Kırımîzâde Ali Rızâ, Mahmud Celâleddin Pasha (Son-in-law), Mâhir Said (Pekmen), Manyasîzâde Refiq, Mehmed Ali Halim Pasha, Mehmed Reşid Şahingiray, Mehmed Sabahaddin, Mehmed Talat Bey (Pasha), Midhat Şükrü (Bleda), Mizancı Mehmed Murad, Mustafa Râgıb, Mustafa Rahmi (Arslan), Dr. Nâzım, Nuri Ahmed, Ömer Nâci, Said Halim Pasha, Sâlih Cemal, Sâmipaşazâde Sezâi, Selim Fâris, Silistreli Hacı İbrâhim Paşazâde Hamdi, Tarsusîzâde (Müftüzâde) Münif, Tunalı Hilmi, Yusuf Akçura.

The common point of Young Turkishness and Young Turks was discontent with ruling of Abdulhamid II and the desire to overthrow this administration and establish a constitutional regime.

The newspapers they published were influential in the dissemination of the names and ideas of Young Turks. Heavy censorship applied on the Ottoman press in order to prevent the disinformation, prevent sedition from being spread among the people and articles written against the sultan had increased the interest in the Young Turk press. Actually, Ottoman political ideas and debates during 1878-1908 had occupied this press. All kinds of topics from organizational arrangements to religious articles, from revolutionary themes to intellectual discussions were processed in more than 100 Young Turk journals.

One of the first names that comes to the mind when Young Turks are mentioned is Mustafa Fâzıl Pasha, grandson of Mehmed Ali Pasha. Pasha would be one of the biggest supporters of the Young Turks with an inheritance worth two-and-a-half million in gold.

After working in leading positions in Istanbul such as the Ministry of Finance and working with the Reformists, Pasha was dissatisfied and went to Paris. In Paris, he started to publish publications against the regime. A group of young intellectuals (Ziya Pasha, Namık Kemal, Ali Suavi, Mehmed Bey, Nuri Bey, Reşad Bey, Agâh Efendi) gathered together in İstanbul

Ziya Pasha (on the right), a powerful poet and a regretful rebel

to establish a secret society and when their meetings became and investigations started Mehmed, Nuri and Reşad fled to Europe. Subsequently, Ziya Pasha, Namık Kemal, Ali Suavi and Agâh Efendi also fled to Paris. Those who fled from Istanbul gathered around Mustafa Fâzıl Pasha. Pasha allocated all of them high salaries. These young intellectuals, who produced various newspapers and engaged in political activities in Europe, spread the name of the New Ottomans, wrote many articles and produced books.

Before long, Mustafa Fâzıl Pasha's reached an understanding with the government and returned to Istanbul and was appointed minister. The Pasha continued to pay the salaries of the New Ottomans for a while. Soon afterwards the New Ottomans returned to the homeland one by one by either by reaching an agreement with the government or by taking advantage of the general amnesty. They did not hesitate to take up civil service in the administration they had criticized so vehemently. Ali Suavi was involved in revolutionary movement named the Ciragan Incident and died.

Although the staff that formed the core of the New Ottomans was dispersed in this way, their opinions, constitutionalism and democracy would spread increasingly.

THE ORGANIZATION THAT DEMOLISHED THE STATE: COMMITTEE OF UNION AND PROGRESS

Through spy Lawrence the British clandestinely fanned the flames of Arabism, and did the same with the Serbs with spy Seton-Watson as well as the Albanians with Lady Dunham, they stirred up Bulgarian nationalism with Noel Baxton carried out a finely tuned study to break the Ottoman Empire into pieces.

Lord Buxton, the British statesman who sided with the Bulgarians and indirectly led the Empire to destruction

Even though Sultan Abdulhamid's actions prevented the collapse, the admiration for the West had spread and morale had collapsed. Russia increased its demands for Armenian reclamation, and the United Kingdom, in addition to the territories seized by Cyprus and Egypt, had penetrated into Ahru'l-Ghazal, Kerdifan and Darfur. The French confiscated Madagascar in 1890, as they had settled in Tacura and Tunisia, and had taken over Morocco. The Italians had turned Masu, Eritrea, Ra's al-Hafun, and Somalia into colonies. Austrian Hungarian Empire occupied Bosnia Herzegovina.

In addition to these negative developments outside the country, the worsening economic conditions would cause the opposition to become progressively louder.

The first opposition that emerged with political demands against the administration in the reign of Sultan Abdulhamid II was the Young Turks who had been groomed during the reign of Sultan Abdulaziz. The second strong current was initiated on June 3, 1889 by Istanbul Tıbbiye-i Şâhâne (Military Medical School) student Arap Cevik, Arapbek, İshak Sükûî, Ohrili İbrahim Temo and Kafkasyalı Mehmed Reşid and Bakülü Hüseyinzâde Ali who founded the "Ottoman Union /Progress and Union". Subsequently, this society, which took the name Progress and Union and operated clandestinely, expanded in a short period of time by infiltrating positions in military schools, the army, and the Sublime Porte's secretariat. When an investigation was started on the news of the activities of the society that propagated against the sultan in 1895, some of the members of the

The entrance gate of the Imperial Military Medical School (Phebus)

society were arrested and some of them fled to Europe. The organization gathered around the opponents of the regime in Europe and wrote articles about the things they were dissatisfied with in an aggressive style. Some of the writers and intellectuals were receiving financial aid from foreign governments.

Divisions incurred in the organization over time. One of them, Ahmet Riza Bey, founded a new organization called the Ottoman Union and Progress Society which started to publish a newspaper called Meşveret as of 1895. In the congress held in 1896, Mizancı Murad Beg, the editor of Mizan newspaper, known for his more liberal views, was appointed chairman of the society. In early 1897 the headquarters of the Committee of Union and Progress moved to Geneva.

Prince Sabahaddin, on the other hand, had established another society under the name of 'Adam-i Merkeziyet-i Idâre and Teşebbüs-i Şahsi'. He was spreading his own ideas with the 'Terakki' newspaper. Prince Sabahaddin offered to connect all the Ottoman provinces as headmen into a confederation at the congress, which he gathered between 4-9 February 1896 in Paris. He urged European states to intervene in order to enable this.

Murad Beg, a famous figure of the Ottoman press

Representatives of all opposition groups attended the congress held in Paris under the leadership of Prince Sabahaddin Bey and Ahmed Rıza Bey. There were representatives of Greek, Armenian, Jewish, Albanian, Arab and Circassian minorities at this congress as well. In fact, the Armenians participating in the congress were delegates of the "Trock" and "Hunchak" revolution committees. They said that they would only cooperate against Sultan Hamid on the condition that Article 61 of the Berlin treaty was enforced. The only goal of Young Turks was to overturn Sultan Hamid's administration. They thought that everything would be remedied with the proclamation of the constitution.

The Young Turks had secured the young officers of the Third Army in Macedonia. The 'Ottoman Freedom Society' was established within the Lodge in Thessaloniki and contact had been established with the Union and Progress Society in Paris. Before long, the Albanian revolution committees joined the Committee of Union and Progress. Thus the Albanians, who initially wanted autonomy followed by independence, had gained important support.

Paris and Macedonia were the headquarters of the Committee of Union and Progress, which had secretly opened branches at home and abroad. Young officers, who had guerrilla warfare experience and who had a close-up view of the committee during the gang's follow-up, were entering the society. In particular, the young officers who graduated from the War Academy were always appointed to this army and the fact that the Third Army had a sort of military autonomy had turned this place in a headquarters of the Young Turks. The formation in Thessaloniki was one of the first. The founders were Post and Telegram Chief Clerk Talât, Military Academy Director Tahir, French teacher Naki, Midhat Sukru from Thesalloniki and Mülazım Omer Naci Bey. Many officers, civil servants and teachers joined them in a short time. The activity of this community was kept confidential. The members endeavored to spread their propaganda by operating in the Lodges.

The Committee of Union and Progress gained strength when important personalities such as historian Murad Bey, Commissar of National Debt Administration also known as Mizancı because he was also the owner of the famous "Mizan" newspaper and Kazım Pasha, commander of the First Division, subsequently to become governor of Skodra and marshall. Just as Sultan Hamid was about to be deposed, the Sublime Porte raided and Sultan Murad or crown prince Reşad Efendi put on the throne the plan had been revealed, many were captured and exiled and some fled to Egypt and Europe. That is how the activity center moved from Istanbul to Paris.

The crown prince Mehmed Reshad

The unique method of struggle for different societies was various newspapers and journals. It was the common methods for attacking and wearing out the Ottoman administration and provoking the people against it. These publications were smuggled into the country through a variety of means and distributed among the intellectuals and even the people. However, since those who generated these ideas were abroad, it was not possible for these groups to take active action.

Abdulhamid Han felt the movement against him, especially in the Third Army zone. Reports sent by the informants were worrying. A special delegation established for verification of the situation was immediately sent to Thessaloniki. Investigation and prosecution began. Many young officers were detained and sent to Istanbul.

However, the Committee of Union and Progress had pulled the pin. Assassinations against the revolutionary movement began. First, they attempted to eliminate Nâzım Bey, the central commander of Thessaloniki, who was acting against them. Nazim Bey, who was wounded with the bullet of Major Enver, moved to Istanbul. Police inspector Sami Bey was killed by the Unionist groups. The artillery regiment imam was shot in Thessaloniki.

After the Sultan applied pressure, Major Enver, a major officer of the Committee of Union and Progress, Resne Zone Commander Officer Niyazi and Officer Eyüp Sabri, General Staff District Governor Salahattin,

Salonika where East meets West. A view of the port of Salonica, once one of the most polygot cities of the world

Enver Pasha, the leading figure of the triumvirate

General Staff Major Hasan Tosun took off consecutively in July 1908 and started guerilla activity. Shortly, Şemsi Pasha, who was sent to Manastır with great powers, was shot to death with a pistol, and then Marshall Tatar Osman Pasha sent after him was abducted.

In this process, the government forces in Manastır and 3500 people joined the guerillas. With the assassinations and several thousand people hitting the hills, a major threat was launched against Istanbul.

Sultan Murad II mosque in Skopje (Uskub) and its Muslim neighbourhood

Six thousand Albanians gathered in Ferizovik, 50 kilometers south of Skopje and sent a telegram to the Sultan and after pledging their 'loyalty' they said that if a constitutional monarchy was not declared immediately, 50.000 Albanians would march to Istanbul. It was obvious that this was not serious. It is rumored that Sultan Hamid, who realized that he had been too indulging with the Albanians was rather saddened by this swashbuckling telegram.

JEWS DEMAND LAND FROM PALESTINE

Until the last quarter of the 19th century, the agenda of the Ottoman State did not include a Jewish-related Palestine issue. Jews continued to live as a comfortable minority on Ottoman territory. They did not have any problems because they were not a majority in the state and did not engage in separatist movements. This situation began to change with the foreigners who wanted to settle in Palestine after the War of 93. Jews began to migrate to Ottoman territory due to increasing anti-Semitism in Europe and the mistreatment of Jews in Romania and Russia. As a result of the decisions taken in the War of 93, thousands of Muslims took refuge with the Ottoman lands and thousands of Jews came with them.

Likewise, thousands of Romanian and Russian Jewish families who came to Istanbul in 1892, 1899 and 1900 were placed in distant areas

Sultan Bajezit, the emperor who welcomed the Jewish immigrants exiled from Europe in 1492

such as Edirne, Cyprus and Mesopotamia. In fact, this migration was done in a systematic and planned way. In fact, because of the financial and political crisis of the Ottoman Empire in the 1870s, there were rumors that various circles that were interested in Palestine would open Palestine to Jewish immigration if the Ottoman state was given credit. Already from that time on, Jews began to establish agricultural settlement centers on Palestinian territory. As a result of the Jewish immigration which was supported by individuals and organizations such as the famous Jewish rich Rothschild, the Colonization Union and Zion Lovers established by Baron Hirsch, around 30 Jewish settlements (villages) were established in Palestine between 1882 and 1908.

The Jews believed that the Palestinian lands were promised to them by the divine power. Theodor Herzl would be the person who turned these beliefs of the Jews a political movement. Herzl had begun to disseminate his ideas about the Jewish state he had been thinking of since 1895. He spoke of his ideas to various statesmen or wealthy Jews who extended a helping hand to Jews. To this end, he had made diplomatic meetings with German, British and Ottoman statesmen, even visited the Vatican, but had not received very positive answers.

One of his Austrian acquaintances advised Herzl to contact Michael de Newlinski of the Correspondance de L'est newspaper. Through this person, he decided to apply to Sultan Abdulhamid to provide the land for Palestine. Newlinski's relations with the sultan were good enough to allow direct contact. In fact, it was even rumored that he was one of the sultan's informants in Europe. Herzl convinced Newlinski about establishing a Jewish State in Palestine and asked him to mediate.

Herzl was not aware of the importance of Jerusalem's occupation to the Ottoman Sultan and Muslims. He came to Istanbul in mid June 1896. Herzl did not succeed in meeting with the sultan, despite his hard work and efforts to remain in Istanbul for more than ten days. But Newlinski discussed the issue with the sultan several times. He gave the promise that Herzl would pay twenty million pounds in return for Palestine and settle the issues that put the Ottoman State in trouble with the international community. The sultan replied as follows to Newlinski:

"If Mr. Herzl is your friend like you are my friend, don't let him take a second step in this matter. I do not sell land, even an inch, because this country is not mine to sell, it belongs to my nation. My nation has harvested this country with their blood. This will be repeated before it can leave us. The members of my Syrian and Palestinian regiments were martyred one by one in Pleven. All of them remained on the battlefield, not a single one returned. The Turkish state does not belong to me, it belongs to the Turkish nation. I will not part with any of it. Let the Jews put their millions away, when my state is disintegrated, they can seize Palestine for nothing. However, only our bodies can be divided. I cannot allow surgery on a living body."

The Hungarian Turkologist Ármin Vámbéry

Although Herzl could not provide direct support from the major states in Europe, he continued to pursue a political solution while encouraging the financial organization of the Jews. The Zionist Congress, which he had started in 1897, gathered regularly every year. In April 1899, with the death of Newlinski, Herzl was left without a mediator. On his second visit to Istanbul, he contacted the Hungarian Turcologist Arminius Vambery of Jewish origin, a scholar who he believed had influence on the sultan. Vambery succeeded in getting Herzl an audience and Herzl met the sultan for the first time in May 1901 face to face and spent more than two hours with him. Although Abdulhamid Khan expressed his friendly attitude towards the Jews, he never mentioned the issue of Jewish settlements in Palestine.

A native school, Palestine

Herzl, unable to make any progress with his initiatives on Palestine for many years, decided at least to establish Jewish settlements somewhere close to Palestine. In the meantime he was invited again to Istanbul to discuss the consolidation issue. He met with palace clerks and the vizier on 25 July-2 August 1902. In return for his aid, Herzl asked that Jews be allowed to settle somewhere near Jerusalem, for example, in Haifa, but his request was rejected on the grounds that it was strategically important.

In this last meeting, the answer of First Officer Tahsin Pasha delivered from Abdulhamid Han was the repetition of the previous ones. "The Israelites can be admitted to the Ottoman State, provided that they settle in a dispersed way to be appointed by the government, accept Ottoman nationality and fulfill all their citizenship duties."

Sultan Abdulhamid Han declared the whole of Palestine his personal property in the face of these activities of the Jews. He established new railroads and agricultural establishments in Palestine, and commissioned a personal military for in Palestine. Moreover, in order to strengthen the demographic structure here, he settled some Muslims in the Caucasus and the Balkans in Palestine.

Although the Sultan had prohibited the sale of land to the Jews, the application did not realize as desired. In 1891, the Ottoman government

Sultan Abdulhamid's tughra or royal monogram

closed its gates to all the Jews, and in 1892, even though they were Ottoman citizens, they prohibited the sale of land to Jews in Palestine. However, European states opposed this practice. After the Jews had entered Palestine, it was not possible to obtain the support of foreign state agencies that was necessary to remove them. On the contrary, the Jews who understood that they would be expelled from Palestine applied for protection to their affiliated consulates and the Ottoman government could not do anything because of capitulations.

The measures taken by the Sultan in Palestine and the rejection of Herzl's demands would result in Herzl and his friends provoking the Young

Turks, Armenians and Greeks against the Sultan. Sultan Abdulhamid Han knew the plans to establish a Jewish state. He was aware of the fact that the Jews were spreading through the Zionist and Lodge organizations and the plans that they had for the state. Unfortunately, the statesmen who would dethrone him would be fooled by and become their tools.

When the Unionists seized power, they abolished all the decisions of Abdulhamid Han, which prohibited Jewish immigration to Palestine. Relaxed Zionists established the Palestinian Office of the Palestinian Land Development Agency with headquarters in Jaffa.

Jews who increased their influence in Palestine would stand by the British in the First World War, to fight against the Ottomans with legionnaire Jews. The British would publish the Balfour Declaration in response to this service of the Jews and when the Ottoman State withdrew from the region the foundation of the State of Israel would be laid.

In addition, Sultan Abdulhamidid, who saw the practices in Palestine and the invalidity of the policies executed by the Union and Progress Committee, told his doctor Atıf Hussein: "I am sure that they will succeed in establishing their own state in Palestine over time." in the second year of his dethronement (1911).

SECOND CONSTITUTIONAL MONARCY DECLARED

As can be understood from the statements, the Macedonian revolution of 'Union and Progress' consisted of the racket made by a few assassinations, a few gang demonstrations and the loudmouthing of several thousand Albanians gathered in Ferizovik. If Sultan Abdulhamid had decided to deploy a few Anatolian battleships to the other side, the situation could have taken a different turn. However, nature was taking its course.

Abdulhamid Han was about to be 66 years of age at the time. His reign had lasted 32 years. He had lost his former fitness due to his advanced age and some illnesses. In the memoirs of Tahsin Pasha, when he received bad news from Macedonia, he had said, "I will go with the flow!".

The telegram that saddened him the most among the telegrams he received from the gang chiefs who had taken for the hills, the 'Union and Progress' centers in Thessaloniki and Manastir centers and some military and administrative authorities was the telegram of Rashid Pasha from the Manastir center. The ruler of Serez, Reshid Pasha, said that allegiance would disavowed if the constitution was not declared immediately.

The first secretary of the Sultan, Tahsin Pasha

All these telegraph were collected from the Assembly and piled in the palace, but the Sultan's thinking was not yet known. Chief Clerk Tahsin and Clerk Arab İzzet Pasha were with the sultan and according to the memoirs of Tahsin Pasha, Sultan Hamid stared fixedly into the distance and finally said to İzzet Pasha:

'The proclamation of the constitutional law was in my time. I established it. It is necessary to declare a recess for a while. Go to the Council of Ministers, tell them and declare my will for the writing of a mandate! Thus, it was decided to re-declare the constitutional monarchy. The Council of Ministers mandate was written and dispatched to all independent province directorates in the evening as well as the Istanbul press with an official notification.

With the proclamation of the II. constitutional monarchy July 24, 1908, the sultan would open the assembly he closed on February 13, 1878, re-enact the suspended constitution. Unfortunately, there were not enough committed people to apply it. The Unionist soldiers were only a few low ranking officers. It could not be expected that these young people who gained fame by fighting with Greek Turkish and Bulgarian gangs in Rumelia could rule the state.

Bulgarian revolutionary Apostol Petkov, seated in the center of the front row

Shortly after the proclamation of the constitutional monarchy, the headquarters of the committee was transferred from Thessaloniki to Istanbul. Immediately upon the declared general amnesty, the opponents in various parts of the country began to return to Istanbul with the Young Turks. The officers, who came off the mountain and were all treated as national heroes, and their fame spread all over the state. Even the 'decentralist' Sabahaddin, who made propaganda for the fragmentation of the Ottoman Empire into local autonomies for years, did not hesitate to come to the country with the attitude of a national hero and was greeted with fervent cheers. Throughout the country, unconscious joy had occurred with the influence of the propaganda carried out. Crowds of people were all around, they cheered with flags in their hands. A large crowd of people and students from the Medical School, gathered in front of Yıldız Palace and chanted, "Long live the sultan". The Sultan was not so innocent as not to know that this was commissioned with the distribution of money. On the insistence of the people to see him, he saluted the people from the window of the palace and made them disperse.

Sultan Abdulhamid Han said the following to those in the palace:

"I have witnessed a desire among the people for a constitutional administration, therefore I have summoned the assembly to a meeting without waiting for the council of ministers decision. I promise you that I will never lift the constitutional law and maintain it as long as I am in power and

Prince Sabahaddin, the man who maintained decentralization was the mandatory choice to keep the empire firm; it proved not be so though

I want you to inform everyone of this. I hope our Council of Ministers will do good deeds for our state and nation and ensure all peace in our homeland. May the Almighty deem us successful in our deeds."

The proclamation of the constitutional monarchy caused many manifestations all over the 'Ottoman country', the embracing of turbaned teachers and priests and Christian gangs descending from the mountains of Macedonia and joining Ottoman demonstrations (coalescence of the elements). However, in reality neither the Bulgarian, Serbian, Greek or other gangs had given up on national causes. Their joy was the manifestation of an environment where they would be easier to achieve.

All kinds of freedom and all kinds of peace were promised to the public. The press was suddenly released from censorship. "Cemiyyet-i mukaddese", (Sacred Society) which was unknown at the beginning of this first drunken atmosphere, was acclaimed and 'Union and Progress' branches started to be established everywhere. No one had felt the necessity to look up the meanings of such dazzling words as freedom, justice, equality, brotherhood, the new terms spread immediately among the people. For example, the term 'Cemiyyet-i mukaddese' meant 'Ottoman Union and Progress' which is considered 'Münci-i millet' (Savior of the Nation). The Ottoman army was "Nigehbân-ı hürriyet (Guardians of Freedom). The city of Thessaloniki, where headquarters was located, was named "Mehd-i hürriyet" or "Kâ'be-i hürriyet" (Qibla of Freedom). On the other hand, the period of absolutism between the two constitutional monarchies was called "Devr-i istibdad" (Despotic Reign) or "Devr-i sâbık" (Former Regime). "Kahramân-ı hürriyet" or "Mücâhid-i hürriyet" (Heroes of Freedom) were the titles given to Officer Niyazi, Major Enver and Officer Eyyub Sabri Efendi who took to the mountains.

Jamal Pasha

Eight days after the proclamation of the constitutional monarchy, a telegraph was published in Istanbul newspapers from the headquarters of the Union and Progress Committee in Thessaloniki. It wrote that the constitution of the society had been achieved, that it endeavored to deliver full benefits of the concessions of this regime and that a special delegation consisting of society members Staff Major Jamal (later Minister of the Navy Jamal Pasha) Hakkı bey (Hafiz Hakki Pasha in the future), Necib, Talât (Minister for Internal Affairs and Vizier Talat Pasha in the future), Rahmi (future governor of Izmir), Javid (Minister of Finance and Public Administration) and Hussein Bey had been dispatched to Istanbul to preserve and develop the faith and trust between the community and the government and help the nation benefit from the fruits of the newly-established regime. The members of this delegation met with the grand vizier in the Sublime Porte. After a while, they became unofficially dominant. Thus, the de facto domination of the Union and Progress had started.

Although the Committee of Union and Progress turned into a political party after a while, they always maintained their capacity as a 'committee' in their organization and continued gang and committee activities. It would be possible for this party to actually take power and seize the government literally only in the First World War when Talât Pasha was transferred to the Grand Viziership. Since the Second Constitutional Monarchy, he had irresponsibly held on to all authority. In the meantime, although some of the members had achieved highest administrative authority, the responsibility of being a government had not penetrated this party. Thus, there would be confusion of authority and responsibility in the state. Even more importantly, irresponsible party administrators would have dragged the country into disaster without thinking of the national situation because of their lack of political experience, administrative knowledge and statesmanship. The sultan's political tactics, with which he had tried to avoid the least damage for thirty-three years by carefully measuring the balance of force between the foreign states and the possible consequences of this, would be shattered by the irresponsible decisions of the new ones and consecutive major losses would follow in this area starting right at the beginning of the constitution...

Sultan Abdulhamid had a detailed manuscript written for the proclamation of the II. constitutional monarchy and had it read on Sunday, August 2, 1908 in the Sublime Porte. The Sultan stated that the Constitutional Law had been proclaimed during his reign, however, as a result of events it was suspended after a while, and now that the constitutional administration had the ability to continue in compliance with the general demand it had been reinstated and that the assembly would convene every year.

Although every class of people can be found equal to one another and cannot be held superior to one another, weakness in these provisions had been observed in some places as well as in state administration and their elimination was declared.

The Sultan opened the second council on December 17, 1908 after a 32-year period. The people of Istanbul gathered in front of the parliament

Talat Pasha (Fourth from right)

in a large crowd. The MPs came to the assembly amidst applause, passing through the ranks of soldiers who were standing on duty. In particular, the arrival of Ahmad Riza Bey, who was struggling with the regime of absolutism, generated fervored cheer. Fifteen minutes later, Abdulhamid Han came to parliament with his royal vehicle and ceremony. In the meeting room after greeting the deputies he remained standing.

Then Grand Vizier Kamil Pasha

Grand Vizier Kamil Pasha gave the opening speech of the sultan to Cevad Bey, the head of Mabeyn. Cevad Bey read the text of the speech aloud. Again he said that the Constitutional Law had been put into effect during his reign, that the state had felt the necessity of its temporary removal from application, now with the spreading level of culture, he was reinstating it despite some opposition, and that together with the declaration of the constitution he unfortunately also declared Bulgaria's independence and Austria's declaration of the annexation of Bosnia and Herzegovina, saying that the government would struggle to defend the rights of the state rights until the end of the government and wanted the assembly to work on this issue. In his speech he also reported that relations with European states were friendly, financial issues would be resolved and a balanced budget would be prepared, citizens would live in welfare, schools would be opened, knowledge and art would be spread, necessary steps would be taken to reinforce the army and navy and that the laws that would enable this would be put before the assembly. Finally at the end of his speech, the Sultan stated in particular that the administration of the country with the Constitutional Law was an integral part of his administration.

A 'carte postale' showing the fervor of the public servants for setting Lady Freedom free!

After the speech was finished Sultan Abdulhamid left parliament before long and returned to the palace.

The Sultan was aware of the fact that the community was not mature enough to undertake Constitutional Monarchy. The structuring of the institutions and the training of the administrators would take time. There was no environment to guide the state administration. The imperfections of the present soldiers and managers were obvious. Recently, they had been instrumental in the activities carried out by foreign states in the field of culture. For example, they were building a stage in the garden of the Ministry of War and having officers undertake roles. He said the following to a palace clerk who invited him to one of these plays:

"This Homeland play is designed to instigate people to revolt. While the misery of people needs to be mitigated and public order maintained, they are still trying to excite the minds of the people. And our officers, our soldiers have become actors and this is not permissible. A soldier on stage? Where is the honor of the military service? If our officers are seen as actors in theaters, the Turks will never respect them.

"And what are these clubs? The Arab club, the Albanian club, the Greek club, every nation has made a club for itself. These are bad things. This state is comprised of many different tribes. Efforts should be made

Sultan heading back to the Yıldız Palace after the Friday Procession (Zonaro family archive)

to unite them. Judging by this course, each tribe is preparing to live separately. These things are not so easy, in fact they are very difficult. They will not let me get involved. I don't want to get involved anyway. However, if things go south they won't be fixed. Tell the grand vizier, the pasha, ban the officers, the soldiers from acting in theaters and these clubs. I am saying this in the name of Islam and Turkishness. I will speak to the Grand Vizier myself." (Ali Cevat Bey, Summary of Proceedings, [The Declaration of the II. Constitutional Monarchy and the 31 March Incident, nşr, Faik Reşat Unat], TTK. 1960, p. 14)

It was a fact that, for a lot of separatist elements, which had shed blood for years to leave the Ottoman rule, been supported by the European states in rebellion movements, and legally referred to some articles of the Berlin treaty, the Parliament would become a scene of struggle. This bitter truth was manifested with the first Turkish Parliament. Talat Pasha, one of the people who dragged the state into this game, describes this historical gaff in his memoirs as follows:

"(Young Turks) Arabs, Greeks, Albanians, Turks believed that they could work together for the peace and dignity of the beloved homeland. But unfortunately, the events following the revolution showed a completely different side."

In Jamal Pasha's memoirs, when he talks about the attempts of the society on the proclamation of the Second Constitutional Monarchy to unite with other revolution committees, he says:

'When we talked about the principles of Ottomanism, the Bulgarian revolutionaries did not want to sacrifice even a small part of the idea of Macedonia's autonomy. Only God and we know how we suffered during these negotiations that we were authorized to carry out with Talat Bey..."

The other problematic aspect of the Second Constitutional Monarchy was that the revolution that caused the proclamation was not a national and public movement, but a mere gang and committee movement with a territorial and military nature. Therefore, the Balkan committee, which considered the constitutional monarchy as its own property, dominated the state as it wished They put politics into the army and immersed the Sublime Porte in a spirit of gangs, accelerated the collapse of the state and established an oligarchy under the name of 'Constitutional Monarchy' instead of a monarchy.

The constitutional government was declared, elections were held and the assembly was called to the meeting. This unexpected development surprised the Unionists. They did not trust the Sultan, they feared that they

Fausto Zonaro; commissioned painter of the Sultan

would be sent into exile at the first opportunity. Aware of this situation, Palace clerk, Ali Cevad Bey, suggested that the sultan should give a reassuring speech to the deputies in the opening ceremony of the assembly. This was because most of the deputies themselves or their first degree relatives had been sent into exile by the sultan for trivial reasons. After the opening speech, Sultan Abdulhamid said the following:

'Those that have been exiled have been exiled in the name of the law. I personally bear no ill will against anyone. They are harmless. However, I must insist on the security of the people. Insecurity is a bad thing. While all European states are governed by Law, I knew that my old administration would no longer be possible and I was waiting for the right time. They wanted Constitutional Law. I gave it gladly without hesitation. Even if I die, I will not change my mind. (Summary of Proceedings, p. 28)"

CONSECUTIVE LOSSES

With the proclamation of the Constitutional Law, preparations for the National Assembly elections began. Union and Progress engaged in activities for the election of MPs from the concessionary states such as Eastern Rumelia, Bosnia and Herzegovina and Crete, which were affiliated with the Ottoman Empire. They even wanted to put Tunisia and Algeria into the election. This, however, would lead to very different results.

On October 5, 1908, when the Ottoman State asked for MPs from Bosnia Herzegovina, the Austrian government announced the annexation of Bosnia and Herzegovina which had been occupied by the Austrians. This was the first result of the political injustice of the Union and Progress.

The second important development occurred in Bulgaria's Eastern Rumelia which was legally attached to the Ottoman Empire and paid taxes each year. The Bulgarian prince Ferdinand was the governor of this province which was legally affiliated with the Ottoman State. After the Union and Progress wanted to choose deputies from here, Bulgaria was worried that it would be attached to the Ottoman parliament, including all Macedonia. On October 5, 1908, they declared their independence.

The careless and ignorant politics of the Union and Progress did not only disrupt the efforts to reach a Turkish-Bulgarian-Serbian, they were instrumental in the establishment of a Greek-Bulgarian-Serbian alliance against Turkey. People were disturbed by these developments. A boycott against Austrian goods and especially fez from there started. However, a few months later the government officially acknowledged that Bosnia and Herzegovina had joined Austria. An agreement in Istanbul also recognized the independence of Bulgaria.

The state had started to disintegrate like a broken rosary. The island of Crete would have its share of this disintegration. The island was a 'privileged island' under the military occupation of Britain, France, Italy and Russia and officially administered by the Ottoman State. The election of a deputy from Crete meant that it would be under the Ottoman State. On October 6, 1908, the General Assembly of Crete declared that the island had joined Greece.

Because of the politics of the Union and Progress in the Constitutional Monarchy, the lands gained at the cost of the blood of martyrs were lost one by one.

The elections would be held regardless of the cost. The election activities took the form of a struggle between Turkish and non-Turkish individuals. Minority churches, pastors, rabbis were spreading propaganda in secret. The Center for decentralization of Ahrar Party was established by Prince Sabahaddin Bey against the Committee of Union and Progress.

17376. P. Z. - SARAJEVO. BENDBAŠI

Sarajevo, Bendbashi. While Bosnia was still Ottoman

Franz Joseph I of Austria

During these elections, the Greek government and the Patriarchate carried out serious activities. According to the Greek press there were six million Greeks on Ottoman territory and demanded that Greek should be an official language together with Turkish.

On the one hand, the gang activity of the Unionists continued. They wanted to win the elections using the army. They put their candidates into all the polls. As a result of the plotting, the Union and Progress gained a majority in parliament. Parliament was opened on 17 December 1908 in the former courthouse next to the Hagia Sophia. There are controversies over different sources regarding the nationality and number of deputies in the Assembly. According to the generally accepted sources, there were 27 Albanians, 60 Arabs, 26 Greeks, 14 Armenians, 4 Jews, 4 Bulgarians, 3 Serbs, 1 Vlah, 1 Maruni, 1 Druse deputy. Turkish MPs were in minority.

Faced with this situation the Sultan is reported to have said he following to Tahsin Pasha:

"The interests of a country are of primary interest to a ruler, if interests require the declaration of Constitutional Law then this will be done, however, whether or not it will be implemented well, whether the rights of the Turks will be reserved, that I do not know. It is never to the benefit of the homeland when elements with various agendas congregate, where factions debate. This has been bitterly experienced in Parliament."

When the assembly opened, no party had been established in the name of Union and Progress yet. The Unionist leaders engaged in military service did not have any influence in Istanbul. (The first four congresses held in 1908, 1909, 1910 and 1911 were secretly held in Thessaloniki and the members of the Central Committee were not made public.) The attempt of a secret society to direct power without carrying political responsibility would face harsh criticism.

Unionist sympathizers the Ministers of Defense and Admiralty were dismissed to keep Grand Vizier Kamil Pasha, the enemy of the Unionists, away from state affairs and keep politics from the military and replaced with names in their favor. The Sultan also approved these procedures. Kamil Pasha wanted to remove the Hunter Battalion, which was the guarantor of the Unionists in Istanbul, from the capital. The Unionists, who saw this situation as a threat to them, mobilized the assembly and gave the government a vote of no confidence. On the day that the deputies were replaced, Nâzım Bey, one of the prominent leaders of the Union and Progress Party, rushed to the mansion of the Grand Vizier and told him that the Society considered the change strange and asked how this was done without giving them notice. Kamil Pasha responded calmly by saying that there was nothing strange

Hagia Sophia

in this matter. As a result the Union and Progress decided to get rid of Kamil Pasha. Immediately, messengers were dispatched to Edirne and Thessaloniki with news that the government wanted to bring back the autocratic administration to provoke the officers of the second and third armies. They immediately sent a flurry of telegrams to parliament and other places saying that they would act at once. The navy officers also informed that they did not want Hüsnü Pasha and that they would not recognize any other authority than the assembly. All these telegrams were read in an agitated session and it was argued that the country was in anarchy. After going back and forth to Yıldız Palace, the government resigned and the sultan appointed Hussein Hilmi Pasha as grand vizier.

The two months between the time Hussein Hilmi Pasha was appointed Grand Vizier until April 13 (Rumi 31 March) was a period of violent political struggle between the Union and progress members and the opposition. At the end of this, the famous reactionary insurrection would take place to be followed by the dethronement of Abdulhamid Han.

The work of the West, which fostered ethnic separations, was facilitated with the atmosphere of constitutionalism. The Bulgarians, Albanians, Armenians and Greeks were out of control. Clubs, societies, associations, newspapers, magazines were issued one after the other. Serbesti, Volkan, Mizan and İkdam newspapers were making all kinds of provocations and even those who claimed that parliament should be closed again were encountered.

Hussein Hilmi Pasha, looking over the shoulder of Said Pasha on the left

The sultan, who was disturbed by the unrestricted publications of the newspapers, said the following to the chief clerk:

'These newspapers take every opportunity to blame me for every evil deed in the past and present. I have been the ruler until now. Now I will reign the execution of the ruling constitution.

'The people asked me for the Constitutional Law. I delivered it right away. I was already aware that an autocratic administration in my country was not possible in the middle of Europe. Was I at fault for doing this? If every ruler who gave his people Constitutional Law were abused like this, no ruler would comply with this.

"In the first days of the revolution Ragıp Pasha spoke about the seriousness of the situation and told me that I should flee to Europe. However, I never accepted abnegating my nation and country. I will never flee regardless of the cost to me. Let them destroy me here. I delivered the Constitutional Law, I will not go back on my word. These journalists are a strange breed, until 5-10 days ago they demanded and received salaries and allowances from the palace. They should show some kind of prudence.

This Serbesti newspaper is the newspaper of our Big Brother. Mevlânzade Rifat is their man. The Brother has a chief clerk. He is a very intelligent and able man. He always handles these newspapers. You do not do anything. This will not do. Both here and in Europe, journalists are blackmailers. When I complain about them they say all sorts. Our enemies keep busy. We don't do anything. They give money to these papers. You are a decent man, I'll give you a few hundred lira; keep you with me. When these journalists come to you, give them an appropriate amount of money to act with discretion. It is time you try to close the mouths of these guys. (Summary of Proceedings 40)

THE THREE ERAS OF UNION AND PROGRESS

Historian İsmail Hami Danişmend divides the power of the 'Union and Progress' committee, which had become a party, into three phases during the nearly ten years from 1908 to 1918:

The first phase lasted for 9 months, 5 days coinciding with the proclamation of the Second Constitutional Monarchy on Thursday, 23 July 1908 until 27 April 1909 when the Operations Army was dispatched to Istanbul on the '31 March Incident' to deal with Sultan Abdulhamid and rule the state. During this first phase Union and Progress dignitaries did not participate in the government and were unable to completely demolish the power of the Sultan. The Society was not held officially and legally responsible for this first phase. However, Talat, Javid, Jamal and Rahmi Efendiler

During the March incident at Taqsim (1909)

who were among important dignitaries of the committee and some other friends had come to Istanbul from the very early days of the independence and met with government officials every day and dictated the will of Union and Progress in every issue. In the rural areas, governors and district governors always acted in accordance with the orders of the Union and Progress branches. Moreover, opposition journalists and former henchmen were being shot by clandestine hands in the middle of the street and in darkness corners; political murders were being committed. This first phase, which continued by involving the army in politics and communicating orders behind the scenes, was the irresponsible 'Dominance phase' of the Committee of Union and Progress.

The second phase was the period that lasted for 3 years, 2 months and 19 days from 1909 until 16 July 1912, when the ninth Said Pasha cabinet fell. It is the first official dominance phase of the 'Union and Progress' committee.

The third phase lasts for 5 years, 8 months and 22 days from 23 January 1913 Thursday, the day that coincides with the raid on the Sublime Porte to 14 October 1918 Monday which coincides with the resignation of the cabinet of Talat Pasha on the disastrous result of World War I. It is the 'last phase of dominance' when the 'Union and Progress' committee abolished the Ottoman state.

THE FINAL YEARS OF THE SULTAN

31 MARCH INCIDENT

The order that had been destroyed by inexperienced hands had to be rebuilt. Particularly, Sabahaddin Bey's Ahrar Party, one of the supporters of Reshad Effendi, who was planned to be put on the throne, was carrying out every form of provocation. The Sultan was worried by the grave course and said, 'Chief clerk, by the way these newspapers are attacking the authority and sultanate they will no longer warrant any significance. I think I will be the last sultan.'

The eight months from the proclamation of the constitutional monarchy to that day had passed chaotically under the domination of a clandestine and unofficial committee, which had disappointed the public. Moreover, the political murders commissioned by the committee in Istanbul had created an air of hatred among the people. In particular, the fact that the murderers were not captured was explained as the government's hesitation in terms of justice. These political murders started with the summons of Ismail Mâhir Pasha, a man close to the sultan, to come to Harbiye from his home to be killed by an unknown murderer en route. The last straw was the shooting of Hasan Fehmi Bey, the chief reporter of 'Serbesti' newspaper on the bridge. On the following day of the event, students and the people demonstrated and shouted out "We want justice!" In addition, after the Constitutional Monarchy, about 10 thousand officers were shelved. It was decided that madrasa students should be recruited into the army, which caused the students to cross to the opposition. The fact that the founders and dignitaries of Union and Progress were members of the Lodge already worried the public, the law on the recruitment of madrasa students into the army was interpreted as a blow against religious education.

The principle entrance of the Ministry of War

The Operation Army and looting of Yıldız Palace

In addition to these situations, complaints were lodged by those who were affected by the Committee of Union and Progress members acting as they pleased, the commands of the Committee of Unionist officers, 'Do not see your teachers! Religious matters are not sought in military service. No one except Allah is recognized. Sultans and their entourage are in the hands of the Union and Progress committee!' At the same time, lay officers who were expelled from the army were making negative propaganda showing the students as "infidels".

When the Bosnia and Herzegovina and Bulgarian disasters after the constitutionalism and the Cretan crisis were added to all these, rumors that all these provinces had been sold to the 'infidel' by the society prevailed.

All these and some similar reasons were the basis of the manifestation of the 31 March Incident (March 31, 1325/13 April 1909). The incident started when the Hunter division officers dispatched from Thessaloniki to Istanbul as a "guards of constitutional monarchy" settled in Taşkışla were imprisoned in their barracks. The men were also sent to other barracks and their participation was ensured and as of '31 March = 13 April Tuesday' shots were fired into the sky to declare the act of rebellion.

Sources report the names of three soldiers with the name of Sergeant Hamdi (Çavus), Bölük Emini Mehmed and Kamacı Usta as the leaders

The Taşkışla Barracks of the Ministry of War

of the action. There were many fanatics and regular people from among them. The uprising lasted 11 days until Saturday when the 'Operation Army' from Thessaloniki arrived to suppress the uprising on Saturday morning, 24 April.

On the first day, the rebels marching to the parliament building on the Hagia Sophia square shouted slogans of 'We want Sharia!', some of the deputies wanted to go down and give advice, but they had no effect. The rebels demanded the resignations of the Grand Vizier Hussein Hilmi Pasha as well as Ahmed Rızâ Bey, the chairman of parliament and that the layman officers are returned to duty. Randomly fired bullets led to some accidents, however, the Justice Minister Nâzım Pasha was mistaken for Ahmed Rızâ Bey and was shot in the heart while Lâzıkıyye deputy Emir Şefik Arslan was shot inadvertently.

The uprising action did not stop there. Ali Kabuli Bey who wanted to fire cannons at Yıldız Palace was taken by the sailors of his own ship to Yildiz and killed in front of Sultan Abdulhamid. It is also on record that some young officers were killed because they were madrasa students.

In this confusion, the administrative offices of some newspapers, such as Tanin and Shoura-yi Ummah, were demolished. Grand Vizier Hussein

Hussein Hilmi Pasha, the then grand vizier

Hilmi Pasha went to the palace and resigned and subsequently went into hiding in a house. Furthermore, Parliamentary Spokesman Ahmet Rıza Bey who was not wanted by the army and many unionist deputies went into hiding.

The following day, Tevfik Pasha, trusted for his objectivity replaced Hussein Hilmi Pasha was tasked with forming the new cabinet, Vizier and Dömeke Hero Ethem Pasha was appointed Minister for Defense.

Sultan Abdulhamid Han, was upset at the events that occurred outside his will. For years, he had tried to prevent such confusion and avoid having people at loggerheads. He had not even thought of any unintentional uprising unfolding in his favor. On the first day of the rebellion, he sent his superior commander Majid Bey to the rebels and declared that Sharia would always be respected and that a general amnesty would be declared if they abandoned the rebellion. Although this placated the incidents somewhat, with the influence of provocateurs the rebels continued their action in full force the next day.

The effect of the March 31 rebellion also triggered different movements in the country. The day after the incident, the Armenian uprising took pla-

Edhem Pasha, an Ottoman field marshal and leading figure in the propagation of a new military doctrine

ce in Adana. The Armenians had been getting armed for a long time and led by Bishop Mousheh attacked the Turks. They even slaughtered children in cradles. When the police and soldiers were incapacitated, the Turks had to defend themselves and about 1800 Turks and 17,000 Armenians were killed. The objective of the Armenian committees to rebel was to ensure the military intervention of the European states and to establish an Armenian government in Cilicia. Since these events were portrayed against the Turks in the European press, of course, the Unionists became worried and punished the poor Turks in order not to touch the Armenian murderers who organized the revolution and appear pleasing to Europe.

The March 31 incident had a very dark side in terms of its initiation and order. The most important point is that Sultan Abdulhamid Han had nothing to do with this incident and that the incident had no religious affiliations whatsoever. In fact, according to the results, it is very likely that it was a scenario against the sultan. As a matter of fact, Sultan Abdulhamid Han has been mentioned as the culprit and organizer of this uprising in many of the official and non-official works written so far.

ONE DAY IN THE LIFE OF THE VENERABLE SULTAN

The 34th Ottoman Sultan, who had kept the state alive for 33 years with his political intelligence and strong character, lived a life of a recluse, away from pomp and entertainment.

The sultan was very kind and friendly, and took good care of his health. After he performed his evening prayer he would go to bed early, get up early in the morning, take a shower with cold water, pray, take a stroll in the garden. He would enjoy his coffee, have a simple breakfast with butter, eggs, milk and scones. Subsequently he would start his daily work and receive planned state dignitaries.

The dinner set manufactured in the 'Royal Atelier' used by the Sultan

The Chit Pavilion

In the afternoon, he would rest for an hour or two, and read a book in the Yıldız Library comprised of a collection of over 10 thousand books. Before long he would have dinner, and he would be busy with government work until late at night. The sultan, who was not a big eater, seldom ate with the female sultans. He usually ate at a stand-alone portable table.

The sultan who had avoided bad habits such as alcohol and night life since his youth loathed laziness and slowness, he worked 15 hours on average per day. He had issued standing orders that when an emergency occurred, he was to be waken up regardless of the hour. Only the ladies knew which room the Sultan was sleeping in any given night.

The sultan's bedroom had a screen, and from time to time for some important works, he would summon the palace clerks to his bedroom. Some nights he worked with some statesmen at the Chit Pavilion until the early hours and prepared declarations.

When he found time from state affairs, he would go out into the garden surrounding Yıldız Palace and interest himself in a variety of plants brought from around the world, and sometimes he would be hunt in the woods. He visited his ceramic, carpenter and clock workshops and worked there. He would play with his children with electrically operated small boats in a pool in his private garden.

Prince Abdulqadir Effendi in the arms of the famous painter Sheker Ahmed Pasha

SULTAN ABDULHAMİD IS DETHRONED

The fraudulent 31 March incident was used as an excuse to remove Sultan Abdulhamid from the throne that he had occupied for 33 years. The cadre who carried out this deed was not aware of what they were doing to the country when they dethroned him.

Fethi Okyar, one of the leading figures of the Committee of Union and Progress explains the confusion and chaos during the II. Constitutional period as follows:

"The Union and Progress, which had initially been able to transform the regime from absolute to conditional democracy by proclaiming the Constitutional Monarchy, could not claim power, because they lacked philosophy of government, staff, as well as preparations ... The power was ours in form but a continuation of the former in practice, I will not say it was a return to the former but rather destroying the current one which went off in sparks among the gaps... As Union and Progress we had undertaken the responsibility of both the Constitutional Monarchy and we were the majority party in parliament. The fate of the homeland rested on our shoulders. Actually we were not in power because we did not have the cadre to govern the homeland or the philosophy to compose this cadre."

In Istanbul, the confusion caused by the application of the wrong policies was spreading. The Unionists began to send the forces they gathered in Thessaloniki to Istanbul, arguing that the March 31 rebellion was against the Constitutional Monarchy. Mahmoud Shevket Pasha was the head of the units which were formed by mainly non-Turkish gangs called the Operation Army. The Operation Army seized the outposts on the way from Topkapi and Edirnekapı on 24 April on its way to rescue the ruler from the rebels

The Operation Army, which totaled fifteen thousand invaded the Ministry of Defense. Resistance in Taksim barracks and Taşkışla was broken with heavy gunfire. Meanwhile, the gangs had already arrived at Yıldız Palace. They occupied the palace and attempted to plunder. The commanders of the I. Army asked permission from Abdulhamid II to break up these makeshift forces. The Sultan told his soldiers the following:

"A thousand people will not burn for the sake of one. Two brothers don't shoot each other. I don't want anyone getting hurt. I am the Caliph of Islam, I will not have a Muslim fight against another Muslim. Anyone who wants to use a firearm can shoot me first and then start shooting his brothers in arms." And thus he prevented conflict.

The leading figure of the late period, Mahmoud Shevket Pasha

Mahmoud Shevket Pasha came to Istanbul and took charge of the situation. Martial law was declared and most of the people who were arrested were hanged without being investigated at any length. The rioters, the demonstrators had already disappeared. According to our sources on recent history the March 31 incident was a joint organization of Germans and British Freemasonry. The plan was made by the Masonic lodges in Thessaloniki, the local Masons had provoked it and was put into practice by mercenaries.

When the Operation Army arrived at San Stefanos, some of the ministers and most of the deputies in Istanbul immediately went there. On Thursday (April 22nd), they signed a secret session with the presidency of the former Grand Vizier Said Pasha, who was the chief of the Assembly, affirming that they approved the movement of the army and that they were united with them. Sultan Hamid's fate was initially decided in this session, even a draft fatwa had been prepared. Ahmad Pasha of the Assembly in the Parliament, as previously agreed, offered to resolve the issue of the sultan. After this offer was accepted, it was decided to ratify the case decision based on the fatwa.

Elmalılı Hamdi Effendi (Yazır) wrote the first manuscript of the sultan's resolution fatwa. The fatwa officer Haji Nuri Effendi, who was invited to parliament, did not want to sign this fatwa after reading it. When asked why he didn't sign it, he said that Sultan Abdulhamid Han had not committed the crimes charged to him in the fatwa. The reasons stated in the text of the fatwa were entirely lies and slander. These crimes were cited

Ahmed Tevfik Pasha, the last grand vizier of the empire

as causing the 31 st of March incident, ransacking and burning religious books, wasting the state treasury. In the end, the text of the fatwa was signed after convincing Nuri Effendi and making some changes in the text.

With this fatwa Sultan Abdulhamid Han was accused of untrue fabricated crimes, the decision was based on this fatwa. Later, as some would admit, the Unionists knew that the text in the fatwa was not true. As a result of the hatred and loathing of the sultan, plans were being prepared one by one in clandestine dark corners.

When the Operation Army came to Istanbul, Sultan Hamid made the following offer to Tevfik Pasha, who was in the Viziership:

"Since they don't want me, I can forfeit my reign to my brother; he can administer the state. However, a commission, a parliament, or whatever you say must be established to manifest whether I am involved in this case or not!"

Resim 10: Tevfik Pasha was an Ottoman-born statesman of ethnic Crimean Tatar origin. He was the last Grand Vizier of the Ottoman Empire

Although Tevfik Pasha took this proposal to Head of Assembly Said Pasha verbally, he became anxious and said:

"But what if he is acquitted, then what happens to us?" and refused the initiation of an official investigation.

A four-person delegation was sent to the Yıldız Palace. They would report that Sultan Hamid was dethroned. One of these four people was Minister of the Navy Arif Hikmet Pasha who had been the adjutant of the Sultan for a long time and worked with an Italian spy and Jewish MP Emanuel Karaso of Thessaloniki who would instigate the Armenian insur-

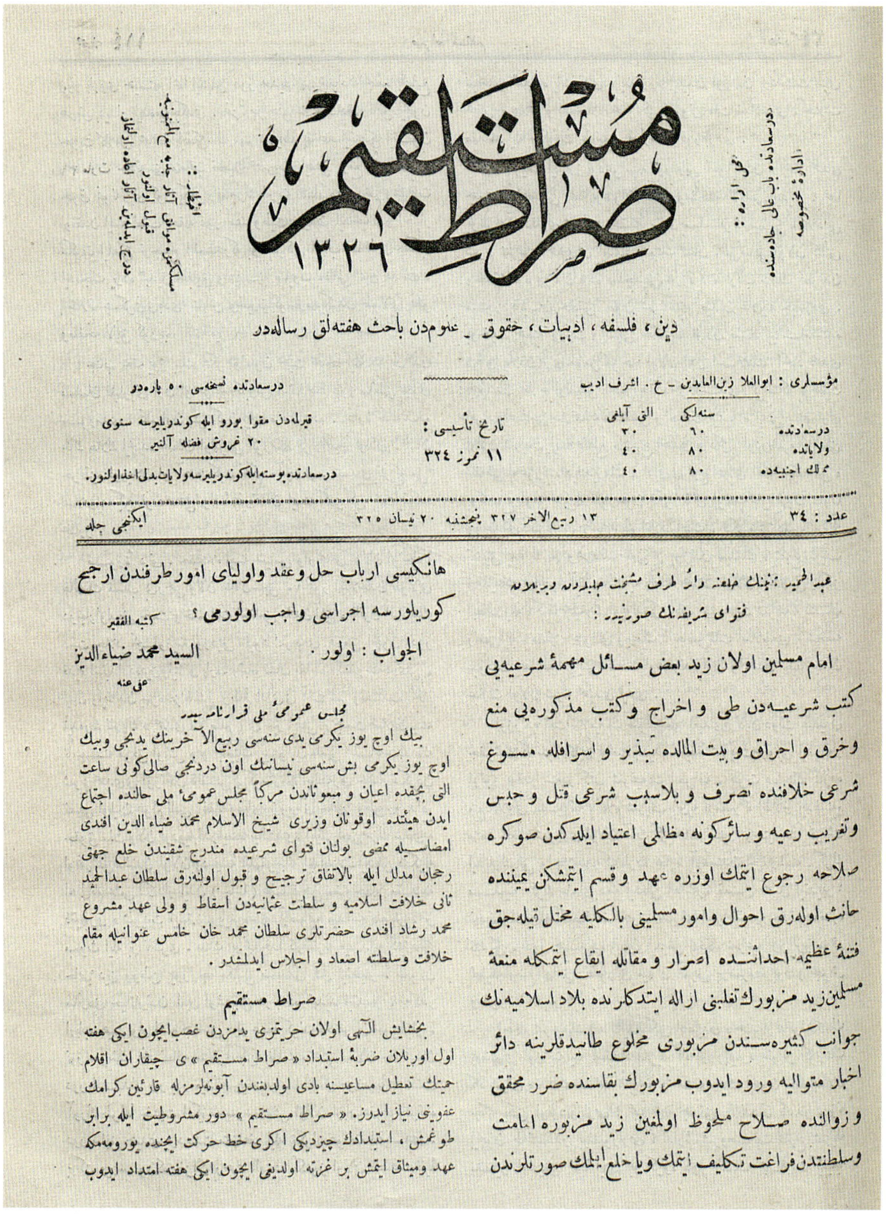

صراط مستقيم
١٣٢٦

دين ، فلسفه ، ادبيات ، حقوق ـ علومدن باحث هفته‌لق رساله‌در

مؤسسلری : ابو العلا زين العابدين ـ ح . اشرف اديب

	سنه‌لكی	التی آیلغی
درسعادتده	٦٠	٣٠
ولاياتده	٨٠	٤٠
ممالك اجنبيه‌ده	٨٠	٤٠

تاريخ تأسيسی : ١١ تموز ٣٢٤

درسعادتده نسخه‌سی ٥٠ پاره‌در

قيرله‌دن مقوا بورو ايله كوندريليرسه سنوی ٢٠ غروش فضله آلنير

درسعادتده پوسته ايله كوندريليرسه ولايات بدلی اخذ اولنور .

عدد : ٣٤ ١٣ ربيع الآخر ٣٢٧ پنجشنبه ٢٠ نيسان ٣٢٥ ايكنجی جلد

عبدالحميد ثانينك خلعنه دائر طرف مشيخت جليله‌دن ويريلان فتوای شريفه‌نك صورتيدر :

امام مسلمين اولان زيد بعض مسائل مهمهٔ شرعيه‌يی كتب شرعيه‌دن طی و اخراج و كتب مذكوره‌يی منع وخرق و احراق و بيت المالده تبذير و اسرافله مسوغ شرعی خلافنده تصرف و بلاسبب شرعی قتل و حبس وتغريب رعيه و سائر كونه مظالمی اعتياد ايلدكدن صوكره صلاحه رجوع ايتمك اوزره عهد وقسم ايتمشكن يميننده حانث اوله‌رق احوال وامور مسلمينی بالكليه مختل قيله‌جق فتنهٔ عظيمه احداثنده اصرار و مقاتله ايقاع ايتمكله منعهٔ مسلمين زيد مزبورك تغلبنی ازاله ايتدكلرنده بلاد اسلاميه‌نك جوانب كثيره‌سندن مزبوری مخلوع طانيدقلرينه دائر اخبار متواليه ورود ايدوب مزبورك بقاسنده ضرر محقق و زوالنده صلاح ملحوظ اولمغين زيد مزبوره امامت وسلطنتدن فراغت تكليف ايتمك ويا خلع ايلمك صورتلرندن هانكيسی ارباب حل وعقد واوليای امور طرفندن ارجح كوريلورسه اجراسی واجب اولورمی ؟

الجواب : اولور .

كتبه الفقير السيد محمد ضياء الدين عفی عنه

مجلس عمومی ملی قرارنامه‌سيدر

بيك اوچ يوز يكرمی يدی سنه‌سی ربيع الآخرينك يدنجی وبيك اوچ يوز يكرمی بش سنه‌سی نيسانك اون دردنجی صالی كونی ساعت التی بچقده اعيان و مبعوثاندن مركباً مجلس عمومی ملی حالنده اجتماع ايدن هيئتده اوقونان وزيری شيخ الاسلام محمد ضياء الدين افندی امضاسيله ممضی بولنان فتوای شرعيه مندرج شقيندن خلع جهتی رجحان مدلل ايله بالاتفاق ترجيح و قبول اوله‌رق سلطان عبدالحميد ثانی خلافت اسلاميه و سلطنت عثمانيه‌دن اسقاط و ولی عهد مشروع محمد رشاد افندی حضرتلری سلطان محمد خان خامس عنوانيله مقام خلافت وسلطنته اصعاد و اجلاس ايدلمشدر .

صراط مستقيم

بخشايش الٓهی اولان حريتمزی يدمزدن غصب ايچون ايكی هفته اول اوريلان ضربهٔ استبداد « صراط مستقيم » ی چيقاران اقلام حيتك تعطيل مساعيسنه بادی اولدبغندن آبونه‌لرمزله قارئين كرامك عفوينی نياز ايدرز . « صراط مستقيم » دور مشروطيت ايله برابر طوغمش ، استبدادك چيزديكی اكری خط حركت ايچنده يورومه‌مكه عهد وميثاق ايتمش بر غزته اولديغی ايچون ايكی هفته امتداد ايدوب

Copy of the fatwa issued for the dethronement of Sultan Abdulhamid

rection before long with one Draç deputy Esad Toptani, and Aram Effendi of the Armenian committees in the Assembly. When the Sultan found out who had been tasked with the notification he regretfully said the following:

"Couldn't they find someone other than a Jew, an Armenian and an ingrate to notify the Turkish sultan who has reigned for thirty years as an Islam caliph about the dethronement decision?"

Sultan made the following comment to Esat Toptani reading the dethronement fatwa:

"I swear I have no fault, by God I am not guilty, I swear I have no fault, by God I am not guilty. However, unfortunately this is my fate. God damn those who caused this misery. My services are evident. I will not mention them, they will go down in history. After my accession I lifted the death penalty. After all my mercy and good intentions I encounter insults. That is my destiny. Even in this incident I worked hard to avoid bloodshed. I tried, what can I do. My God protect my nation, my homeland. No harm done. All I say is God damn those who caused this evil."

The Sultan calmly welcomed this decision. Subsequently he informed that he wanted to live in Ciragan Palace. Although this wish was granted and promised, he was rushed out of the city immediately that night. Without the need to consult with anyone, Mahmoud Shevket Pasha had put Sultan Abdulhamid on the train from Sirkeci station to Thessaloniki that night and told the assembly the next day that the army had requested this and nobody questioned it. There was anxiety about the Sultan taking the throne again. The Sultan had to be removed from the capital as soon as

The delegation that informed the Sultan he was robbed of his crown (Arif Hikmet Pasha, Emanuel Carasso, Esad Toptani, Aram Effendi)

possible. Sending him into exile in Thessaloniki where the Committee of Union and Progress and the Third Army rules was deemed appropriate.

Years after the death of the Sultan, Attorney Abdurrahman Şeref Laç visits Rıza Tevfik, one of the most famous unionists in Haydarpaşa Public Hospital together with a delegation for another legal matter. They are accompanied by a judge as well. Lawyer Laç asks Rıza Tevfik to tell the inside story of March 31, gets the following answer from him:

"Judge Bey! Judge! We are sinners, sinners, sinners! What reaction, what Sultan Hamid's plot? We did 31 March, it was us! The Union and Progress party did it! May Allah forgive us! May Allah forgive us! May Allah forgive us! If Sultan Hamid wanted it, he would criticize us immediately. But he didn't. His mercy stopped him. He did not want bloodshed. But we did. We've committed murders. May Allah forgive us! Yes, we did it, then we overthrew Sultan Hamid and palace treasure was robbed. Trays of diamonds were transferred to the Union and Progress Center. They were up for grabs and did not do anyone any good...

"Judge, God forgive us, our sin is great. I told Talât Bey that it was necessary to avoid this situation when the fictious 31 March revolution was being prepared. I said it was a great murder to shed the blood of brothers for nothing. The answer I received was: What should we do, Rıza Bey, the Union and Progress Society needs money. This need can only be countered from the wealth of Yıldız Palace and the treasure there.."

Interior view of the royal library in Yıldız Palace that was hardly exempted from pillage

THESSALONIKI DAYS

The Sultan was taken to Alatini Pavilion in Thessaloniki, where he would spend 3 years, 6 months and 3 days of his life. Sultan Abdul Hamid, who was removed from Yıldız Palace with a few suitcases without any belongings in the middle of the night moved to Thessaloniki with his family and 38 people of his entourage. Among them were four women, small princes Abdurrahim and Âbid Effendis and Şadiye, Ayshe and Refîa sultans, many assistants, a few eunuchs and some loyal servants. Major Fethi Bey was the responsible officer of the forty Thessaloniki gendarmerie who were guards. The sad group reached Thessaloniki Kılkış station on 28 April Wednesday after the call to evening prayer and were driven with 15 private vehicles to Alatini pavilion accompanied by a cavalry platoon. The sultan was not given any money for his upkeep in Thessaloniki.

The sultan, who had ruled the state for 33 years, was taken to a place without his consent, without giving any assurance regarding his assets, without any judgment or justification as if he was an enemy of the state. Not only was the Sultan not allowed to take anything, the money and valuables of the palace and its members were plundered by Unionists and soldiers. His personal fortune, gold in banks, stocks and bonds, and cash were confiscated. The Union and Progress did not instigate any investigation as to what happened to the real estate that belonged to the sultan, some of which belonged to the state or who kept them.

The Alatini Pavilion, where the Sultan was removed with a few suitcases without any belongings in the middle of the night

Alatini Pavilion, allocated for the residence of former sultan, was one of the most beautiful pavilions of Thessaloniki. However, the pavilion was almost turned into a prison, and the windows were shut with wooden blinds. The sultan and his staff were forbidden to go outside and into the garden of the mansion, to accept guests and to talk with their relatives. They were not allowed to read daily newspapers and magazines. Sultan Abdulhamid who transformed the first floor of the pavilion into a carpenter's workshop and began to practice his beloved profession was accompanied by four wives and two of his six sons and three of his five daughters. As they were forced to leave Yıldız Palace immediately, they wanted their other children who could not come because they were not present at the palace at the time to join them and continue their education. Furthermore, he was still anxious about his life.

The Unionists decided to confiscate the personal wealth of Abdulhamid which was a major fortune in the name of the army. They sent the paperwork to the Sultan to sign in Thessaloniki. They wanted the personal fortune of the former ruler for which he had worked and saved for the army. The Sultan said he would give it willing to the army, but that he also had some wishes. The sultan wanted to buy the Alatini pavilion in his name, provide security for his family members, give freedom to the people in his service, put some of his personal wealth aside in order to maintain his remaining life in peace and officially put his life under security and guarantee.

After Chief Guard Fethi Bey signed and presented the document that these requests would be fulfilled he said, 'Let it all be sacrificed to the army and the navy. Just let them use it wisely. The responsibility is on their shoulders.'

Although the government had taken away all the assets of Abdulhamid, they had not fulfilled any of his demands. On the contrary, they stopped taking an interest in the former sultan.

Sultan Abdulhamid Han recounts this situation in his memoirs as follows:

"The guards did not hesitate to say that if I didn't give the money to the army, the mansion would be held under cannot fire by the Ottoman fleet and that we would all be destroyed. Some of the money I wanted was in bonds, and fifty thousand liras was allocated for the education of my children. There is nothing I would not spare my homeland. I would have gladly given my remaining two cents. However, even our life safety was not guaranteed. Those who had the duty to protect us threatened to fire cannons and kill us."

Ali Fethi Bey [Okyar]

Thus, the great Ottoman Sultan was deprived of his personal fortune. It was later revealed that a large part of the money and jewelry seized in the name of the army went into the pockets of the Unionist leaders.

Ayshe Osmanoglu, the daughter of the sultan, tells the story of her disastrous life in this mansion where the sultan and her family were shut as follows:

"My father was in front, we were behind him when suddenly we go through the big gate of the mansion and find ourselves in the big hall.

The doors were closed right behind us. At that moment, we knew that we had entered a new realm, that we had left the world. We were all sad and nervous. There was no one in the mansion except us. We were staring at each other in the middle of the empty hall. What were we going to do now? What would happen? How would we live in this house? What was this situation that we didn't see, we didn't know, we had never thought about, that had never crossed our minds and dreams?

"We understood that we were imprisoned after such dangerous, exciting, disastrous, exhausting days. This was a bitter truth. The windows were shut with big wooden shutters. Our relationship with the outside was over. We would live here, maybe die here. We were obliged to get a hold of ourselves, to hide our sadness from our father. Since we had had thrown ourselves into this disaster for his sake, we would not spare our love and affection from our father. It was only yesterday that he was the sultan. We kissed his hand then. Today, all of this is gone. But for us, he is as precious as our soul, our reason for living, our father, whom we are more attached to than ever before.

Sitting on one of the two chairs in the middle of the big hall, we surrounded our father who was looking grave. We said, 'father, you are tired. You must rest. Select one of these rooms. We will prepare it immediately. '

He got up and said, 'What should be done, I don't know'. Then he turned to us and said, 'What are you going to do?'. We said, 'father, don't be sad. We will find a solution.'. Yet as we said that we did not actually know what we are going to do.

However, nothing was resolved. There was nothing in sight. We were in a vacuum. One of the girls, Gülshen said, 'Perhaps there is something upstairs.' How could we go upstairs. The stairs were in darkness.

"We were looking for water. We wanted to wash our hands from the filth of the train. There was no soap. There were no candles to go upstairs.

"We had not had anything to eat since we left Istanbul. In fact we had not been eating during the last week in Istanbul. We were barely existing. Our youth gave us strength. We had no cutlery and glassware. There was not a single carpet or rug in the house. We hugged duvets and lay down on boards. One of us lay down in front of every window and door. That is how our first day in Thessaloniki went by." (Ayshe Osmanoglu, My father, Sultan Abdulhamid, p. 159-162.)

THE SULTAN IN BEYLERBEYİ

The losses started one by one as the Committee of Union and Progress undertook administration with full authority. The Italians occupied Tripoli in 1911. One million two hundred thousand square kilometers of territory was lost in Africa, two hundred and fifty thousand square kilometers of land in Rumelia, the Balkan War had started in 1912. Thessaloniki was on the verge of invasion. Gazi Ahmed Muhtar Pasha's government decided to transfer Sultan Abdulhamid Han to Istanbul on the grounds that it would become more difficult to maintain him in Thessaloniki. Sultan Reşad confirmed this decision.

When Abdulhamid Han was informed of the decision to transfer him to Istanbul, he said that his life was of no value since the homeland had been lost and he certainly would not leave. He said that he was no different from any other person now and that he would arm himself and defend Thessaloniki with the troops until he died, 'If I die, I die a martyr. I'm already a dead man! God damned those who made the state what it is!"

On the outbreak of the Balkan War, Abdulhamid Han was brought to Istanbul on Friday, November 1, 1912 with the Loreley yacht sent by the emperor of Germany and settled in the Beylerbeyi Palace. The Sultan would spend the last 5 years, 3 months, 9 days of his life in Beylerbeyi palace after endeavoring to keep the state standing through thirty-three years of ingenious politics and witness the state being dragged into the First World War through a fait accompli.

Preparations by the Balkan Union for battle at Adrianopole during the First Balkan War

Palais de Beylerbey. №121.

Beylerbeyi Palace on the Asian side

When the Sultan was brought from Thessaloniki, he spoke of the Balkan War with Şerif and Ârif Hikmet pashas as follows:

"How to battle with four states? There are ambassadors and military attaches in the embassies. Have they been sleeping so far? Have the four states established alliances without anybody being aware of what is going on? When I was in office, I always tried to put a spoke in their wheel."

As soon as Abdulhamid Han settled in the Beylerbeyi Palace, he gave an order to his chief guard, Rasim Bey. According to the instructions consisting of ninety-one articles, the former Sultan was strictly forbidden from contacting the outside. No one could enter the palace except those who had been issued permits by the guardianship and those who were deputized. This included the children of the former Sultan, close relatives and friends. The two officers who stayed with the former sultan and those in the palace day and night reported all the conversations and even various signals that were made to the government every day.

It was strictly forbidden to approach the palace after a certain distance from land and sea. These strict measures implemented in the Beylerbeyi Palace were increased further. Whenever there was a change of government, the Beylerbeyi Palace was changed immediately and the officials around Abdulhamid were replaced.

Abdulhamid and his family members and employees were living the life of prisoners in Beylerbeyi Palace just like in Thessaloniki. They were not allowed to have anyone come and go to their home, go out and see relatives. The only difference or novelty here was that the former sultan was given daily newspapers and magazines.

When the move of the Sultan from Thessaloniki to Istanbul was considered, his move elsewhere in Anatolia was also on the agenda: the Unionists were worried about World War I when Çanakkale was challenged by enemies. In this respect, the government was planning to take some measures. For example, moving the Sultan from Dolmabahçe Palace, the former sultan from Beylerbeyi Palace to cities in Anatolia to prevent them from falling into the hands of the enemy were among the plans of the Unionists.

Sultan Reşat was a gentle man willing to comply with every government order. In this respect, it would not be a problem to obtain his consent. The difficult question was whether or not the ex-Sultan Abdulhamid Han would consent to moving from Istanbul to Anatolia. This would have to be discussed with him in confidence. In fact, it was necessary to keep it so confidential that even using an intermediary was ill-advised.

Removing the dead from the trenches during the World War I

While Abdulhamid Han was contemplating the wars of Çanakkale and the future of Istanbul, he read in the newspapers that he was going to be transported to Bursa and Sultan Reşad to Konya. He told his personal physician, Atıf Bey, that his nerves were shot and to prescribe him a sedative. His doctor Atıf Bey pretended not to know anything and asked why. Abdulhamid Han said that first he had been dispatched to Thessaloniki, from there to Beylerbeyi and now he was going to Bursa which was a major insult to him and he certainly would not accept.

Some contacts were made by the Grand Vizier Talat Pasha and the Deputy Commander in Chief Enver Pasha with Sultan Abdulhamid. Abid Effendi, the son of the Sultan, summarized this:

' ... The pashas visited my father during the night when no one could see. My parents and the servants were very worried about the sudden and especially late visits! They even suspected that an assassination attempt would be made on the Sultan. They have been shaking in fear. I was with them. I watched the pashas coming from the beach enter my father's room with my heart beating violently. Talat Pasha and Enver Pasha entered the room where my father was. Both of them approached my father, who was a former sultan, respectfully as if he were the ruler of the day. They kissed his hand with an extreme respect which has to be seen to be believed, evening bordering on hypocrisy. I was able to see clearly through the door which was ajar. My father Ablulhamid welcomed them standing up but never proceeded from where he was standing.

"I remember the unexpected visits of those two famous pashas who held the fate of the state at their fingertips and between their lips that day as if it were yesterday, how the sultan had not been surprised with the unexpected extreme reverence over the rules of protocol that could not be foreseen and the way he motioned the visitors to be seated.

'At that moment, without knowing the reason for this visit, I ran to the room where my mother and the other mistress of our Sultan who were in a state of curiosity. I immediately told them what I had seen and told them not to worry. I spoke about the gestures of the Pashas and their excessive respect so excitedly that my mother Najiye Sabiha construed another meaning and said:

'God is great. I hope they invite my sultan to the throne again!'

'However, I know that the pashas sat with my father for a long time. I have forgotten what was offered to those guests at Beylerbeyi Palace that night.

'After the guests were gone, the Women, the Guards and the close servants tried to interpret the results of this visit in their rooms ...

'One day later, we learned that Talat Pasha and Enver Pasha spoke about the possible bad consequences of the war situation in Çanakkale. They explained the plan to take the sultan, my father and the heir to Anatolia. They asked the former ruler for his opinion because of his experience. Afterwards, according to my father, he listened to the pashas with great calm. He told them about his personal opinion and his suggestion as follows:

'I will not move a step from my place and I will not go anywhere. My advice to my brother the sultan is that he never leaves the palace. God forbid, a separation will disrupt the spirit of the army and the nation. If defeat is destined, this move will accelerate it.

'When I was sultan, I always tried to walk on the path of peace with the big nations, that had an eye on our land and wanted to divide our country as well as the Balkan nations. When I left the sultanate I left a great homeland to the new administration. This valuable land has passed into the hands of our enemies. All we have left today is this. If you can not hold onto Çanakkale, this will only serve to place Istanbul into the hands of the enemy.

Turkish soldiers firing from their trenches in the Dardanelles

'My puissant brother's concerns are futile. If it is untouched, I would have made extraordinary arbitration at the time in terms of Çanakkale. No navy can pass there. The same is valid for the Bosphorus. But if such a catastrophe comes to a head, then what the ruler needs to do is not to attempt to escape the throne abandoning his subjects, but give his life in glory and honor under the stones of the capital. When Fatih the conqueror conquered this town from the infidel, the Byzantine Emperor Costantin did not run away, he was capable of showing the courage of dying under the demolished castles. We, as the grandchildren of Fatih cannot be less than Constantin.

'I prefer to go under the soil and die in this palace with their bullets rather than see Istanbul, the apple of our nation's eye and the center of our state conquered by the great Sultan Mehmet the Conqueror and his companions under occupation. As for your advice on my brother (Sultan Sultan Reşat) abandoning Istanbul, this will be a dark spot on our history. I strongly recommend that you forgo this. My only desire is to die here. I ask for the consent of this from my brother and the government."

It was the time when the Sultan was in Beylerbeyi and the First World War was at the threshold. Talat Pasha went to the Beylerbeyi Palace with Sublime Porte Undersecretary Ali Fuat Bey and the Printing and Intelligence Deputy Ercümend Ekrem Bey to learn what Sultan Abdulhamid thought about the main issues of the motherland and the fate of the nation. After explaining the events that had happened to the state, Pasha asked the Sultan for his advice. The Sultan replied in a rather sad way:

'The issues you are talking about are natural events of the individual and tracked path in the face of the magnitude of the issue. I followed a different policy. Bosnia and Herzegovina has been removed from being an Austrian-Russian issue and turned into the Ottoman-Austrian issue. Crete has been removed from being an England-Russia issue and turned into an Ottoman-Greek issue. It is an unforgivable error that you handled the dispute between the Greek-Bulgarian churches in such a way that it led to the Balkan alliance. Furthermore, you have made the Albanians, who have maintained their loyalty to the state through special privileges, open to the provocations of Serbia-Montenegro-Italy. You have endangered the right to decide of the Ministers Assembly by allowing the unification of Turks and non-Muslim groups.

"With all these errors, the political balance that the state was based on was bared. Thus, those who coveted us surpassed each other in their rivalry and sought an opportunity to act before the others. The rivals of those who initiated action waited for the outcome of the events. This war will be won by those who dominate the seas. The natural resources of Germans are limited. We have difficulty defending extensive borders. The reason for this is that we are dependent on getting all our weapons and supplies from the outside.

"If it has become necessary to enter this war, it is imperative to choose a style of fighting on narrow fronts and defending distant places as much as possible with local forces to the extent possible. I am not going to discuss the reasons. However, it is evident that this has not been possible to execute and apply. Thus, it is obligatory to consider the results. You have to admit that you have considered this before. Otherwise, what is the point of asking for ideas when the results have been manifested?"

THE SULTAN'S DEATH

During the last week of his life (5 February), Abdulhamid Han's discomfort worsened. The Sultan had a cold and often complained about his stomach. He was under the supervision of his personal physician Atıf Bey. On February 9, he took a turn for the worse. He had labored breathing. A high volume of blood had accumulated on both sides of his lung, especially in the right lobe. Sultan Vahdettin Han and the Minister for Defense were informed about the state of the Sultan.

He could not be saved despite treatments. He passed away in Beylerbeyi Palace on February 10, 1918 Monday night around three o'clock. He was 76 years old. He is the second oldest sultan after Orhan Ghazi who passed away at the age of 78. He was prepared and shrouded in Topkapı

Imperial gate, Topkapi Palace, Istanbul

Palace and buried in Sultan Mahmud II Tomb. Sultan Abdulhamid maintained consciousness until the last minute and according to his wishes a treaty was placed on his chest, his face was covered with a piece from the Hırka-i Saadet and his body covered with a shroud from Kaaba.

The Sultan was farewelled with a ceremony given to sultans who pass away on the job. His remains were carried on hands from Topkapi Palace to Sultan Mahmud II Tomb. The streets were full of people wailing and weeping everywhere in Istanbul. The last ceremony of the Ottoman sultan, who had served for thirty-four years was performed with reverence. The coffin passed through the tomb door to the accompaniment of shouts of 'Allah, Allah'. Sultan Abdulhamid was lowered into the grave with respect and thirty-three years of Ottoman history ended in a sad way.

HIS TOMB

The tomb of Abdulhamid Han is a building built of cut marble on the right on the way from Sultanahmed to Cemberlitas on Divanyolu which connects Beyazid to Sultanahmed.

Sultan Abdulhamid Han was laid to rest next to his uncle and his grandfather in the tomb built for his father Sultan Mahmud II by Sultan Abdulmecid.

The Mausoleum of Sultan Mahmud II, his son Sultan Abdülaziz and also Sultan Abdulhamid II who died later in 1918

Although the architect of the tomb is a Turk, the head of Ebniye-i Hassa Abdulhalim Effendi, it is possible to see the foreign styles of Ohannes and Bogos masters in the tomb. The octagon mausoleum draws the attention of every human being passing in front of it with its large and high-arched windows, all marble-covered body and flowers, bouquets, leaf carvings high above the window level and a large, wide, imposing dome.

The tomb, which is a few stairs above the road level, is entered through two iron gates, one on the right and one on the left. When you walk on the paved road, you can see the public entrance gate of the tomb on the left, in the opposite direction of Divanyolu. The tomb is reached by passing through a covered corridor with rooms on both sides. While glazed tile, the indispensable decoration of classical Ottoman era tombs is not used in the interior decoration, calligraphy and penmanship works can be seen in abundance.

There are seventeen sarcophagi of different sizes in the tomb. One of the three large ones on the left belongs to Sultan Abdulhamid Han. In addition, his grandfather Sultan Mahmud II and his uncle Sultan Abdulaziz Han rest in this tomb. Some of the tombs are protected by iron bars. In addition to the three sultans, their wives and children are laid here.

THE SULTAN'S PRIVATE WORLD

CHARACTER AND MORALITY

Sultan Abdul Hamid had a sallow complexion, aquiline nose, dark-black beard, cloudy black eyes. He had a slight stoop. His lashes were long, his gaze was sharp. He was extremely curious, cautious and careful. He had a deep voice. His speech was clear.

The sultan was not angry and harsh, but rather benign and compassionate. He had forgiven insults or assassinations against him and never executed a death penalty. He was suspicious and speculative. He was very meticulous and prudent. He was extremely polite, but not overly and flashy.

He was extremely welcoming and generous. He had valuable gifts for his entourage and his deputies, connoisseurs of science and art as well as foreigners.

He was very brave and trustworthy. During the earthquake of 1894, the sultan was in the large ceremony hall of the Dolmabahçe Palace in a meeting with the state dignitaries. While the others were stomping on each other to get out, the sultan did not move, he read some verses and waited with dignity and trust.

He did not like waste. When he succeeded to the throne, he reduced the appropriation of the sovereign office and transferred many of the Royal Treasury mines and assets to the treasury.

The Sultan, who was very fond of cleanliness, especially paid attention to clean hands and sometimes carried a bottle of cologne and offered some to the people around him.

Sultan in his earlier days of reign

HIS SUPERIOR INTELLECT

Sultan Abdulhamid Han was remarkably intelligent. He understood the political issues very well, looked at the issues from different aspects. His memory was strong enough to be encountered in rare people. He never forgot anyone and kept his decisions in his memory for many years. Although in time the sultan developed anxiety because of the negative experiences of previous sultans, he remained far from forgetfulness and his memory remained intact until the end of his life.

Ismet Bey, the stuntman and sultan's foster-brother (Yedikuta Magazine)

RELIGIOUS SENSITIVITY

The Sultan was very scrupulous in complying with the orders of Islam and avoiding its prohibitions. He was very fond of his worship. He was careful not to be without ablution, made his prayers on time, read the Qur'an regularly and practice dhikr. He has also published his will that the people pay attention to worship. He took precautionary measures against the publishing of unlicensed Korans and took necessary measures for the defense of the Ahl as-Sunnah. He struggled meticulously against harmful publications about Islam both inside and outside the country. He was a member of the Qadiri and the Naqshi order. He obscured this aspect and used his milk sibling Ismet Bey as a double in his state and private life. In fact, there is a rumor that this enabled him to make the pilgrimage.

HIS INTEREST IN ANIMALS

The Sultan had a special interest in animals. He kept animals when he was a prince, during his reign and his days in Thessaloniki.

He liked pigeons and white parrots fascinated him. He had a special interest in horses. He loved riding and grooming. He treated his white steed Ferhan like a loyal friend.

In the garden of the Yıldız Palace there was a zoo with many breeds of animals and rare birds. The zoo hosted many of the most beautiful breeds of cats, different birds, ingenious parrots. These animals, which he doted on, were sadly left behind in the looting of Yıldız in 1909 and perished in thestreets.

The furniture used by the Sultan in his study, designed and manufactured by Victor Rimone

HIS READING

The sultan, who had a private library, read a lot and spoke of the harm of not reading, and wanted everyone to read. He would have books translated on European issues by the translation office that he had founded at the palace and scrutinize them. He continued his reading habits until the last days of his life.

He was interested in police-crime stories, murder mysteries and travel stories. İsmet Bey, his milk sibling would read to him in bed. He awarded Arthur Conan Doyle, who wrote his favorite detective novel Sherlock Holmes a silver medal.

HIS PASSION FOR PHOTOGRAPHY

The foundation of contemporary Turkish photography was laid during the reign of Abdulhamid Han. The Sultan used the photograph to follow the goings on outside the palace and learned about the events in every corner of the state this way. The Sultan had news not only on the territory of the state, but from the American continent to Japan. The Sultan had deputized many local and foreign photographers for special jobs.

The cover of the album sent by Sultan Abdulhamid to the Library of Congress, 1884

The photographers were revealing the institutions in the country, opening ceremonies, developing activities before the eyes of the sultan. This way he commissioned the preparation of photograph albums including photographs of almost all of the navy ships, military institutions, state buildings, schools, hospitals, mosques, police stations, watch towers, historical venues, factories, domestic travel of civil servants, tradesmen groups, foreign statesmen.

The Sultan also used photographs as a propaganda tool to show the power of the state. In 1893, he had sent 51 albums of photos taken by Abdullah Brothers to the Queen of England, King of France, and the President of the United States. In addition to the heads of state, the Sultan sent several albums to the British Museum in London and the Library of Congress in Washington. Seventeen of the albums he sent to the British Museum included historical and natural beauties in the Ottoman geography, seventeen of the photographs of Ottoman land and sea troops, fifteen of them included works by students who had been educated in civilian schools and military schools, and two of them included horses reared in the palace.

The 962-album Yıldız Photograph Albums, consisting of 38 thousand 599 frames, is a very valuable collection not only for the Ottomans but also for world photography. These albums qualify as art masterpieces from their printing to their binding.

HIS BODYGUARDS

Abdulhamid had set up a 250-person 'Sogut Hall Company' in Yıldız Palace that he had handpicked. Mehmed Effendi, the commander of the group, and one of his friends used to lie next to the sultan's bedroom. The soldiers who guarded the palace were chosen from among the old Turkish tribes that settled in the Sogut, Bilecik and Eskişehir regions, the cradle of the Ottomans.

The guards that were chosen to this division known for its courage, bravery and honesty were specially selected. The criteria included being members of the Ertugrul Ghazi and Sogut families, good riding skills, praying five times per day, good morals, orderliness, being handsome and have a strong build. The soldiers elected on a voluntary basis swore at the tomb of Ertugrul Ghazi, that they would remain true to the sultan and obey until their last breath. The Sultan used to refer to these soldiers as "my true compatriots".

Asil, one of the Sultan's favourite

HIS CARPENTRY

The Sultan was also a good carpenter. He would make exquisite tables, cupboards, coffee tables, screens, chairs that manifested his delightful taste in the carpentry workshop in Yıldız Palace. His works, such as desk, offices, drawers which he had fine tuned with his carpentry and stylized craftsmanship, are now admired in the palace, in various government offices and in Yıldız Hamidiye Mosque.

HIS NATIONALISM

Abdulhamid Han also gave importance to the policy of "Panturkism". He sent Sheikh Suleiman Effendi, the author of Lûgat-ı Çağatayî and Türkî-i Osmanî to contact the Central Asian Turks in the early years of his reign. On the other hand, when the Shah of Iran, Muzaffaruddin Kajar, came to Istanbul, he was able to lift the ban on Turkish in the schools of Azerbaijan. The Sultan commissioned the investigation of the founding years of the Ottomans, the writing of books and the preservation of old works.

HIS INTEREST IN GLAZED TILE

The Sultan had a special interest in items made of glazed china. He commissioned the manufacturing of rare items in the Yıldız Tiles Factory founded in 1891 in the garden of Yıldız Palace. The interest of the Sultan in art, seeing the Western countries and the desire to bring new technologies to the country and the revitalization of the art of glazed tile and ceramics that have been developed in Anatolia for centuries have been effective in the construction of this factory.

The porcelain produced in the Yıldız Tiles Factory, an imperial factory like Hereke Carpet Factory, was used primarily in the decoration of the palaces, pavilions and mansions built in the recent era and presented to foreign dynasties as gifts.

Yıldız Porcelain Factory, which has a special position among similar ones as a museum-factory, continues to produce porcelain goods.

HIS FAMILY

Abdulhamid Han had 13 wives, 8 were goodwives while 5 were favorite and 3 were mistresses. He spent the last twenty years of his life by sharing a pillow with Müşfika Kadıneffendi. He had 13 daughters and 8 sons

The Entrance of the Tiles Factory in Yıldız Palace

A golden dining set used by the guests of the palace

The goodwives:

- The sultan's leading goodwife, Nâzikedâ Başkadın Effendi (1851-1895), she wed Sultan Abdulhamid in 1863. She was the mother of Prince Mehmed Selim Effendi, Zekiye Sultan and Ahmed Nuri Effendi.
- Bedrifelek Başkadın Effendi (1851-1930), was the second wife of Abdulhamid Han when he was sultan, they wed in 1868.

- Sâfinâz Nûrefsûn Second Goodwife (1851-1915), the sultan's third wife.
- Bîdâr Second Goodwife (1851-1918) was the fourth wife at the beginning of the sultanate. She procreated Nâime Sultan and Prince Şehzâde Abdulkadir Effendi.
- Dilpesend Third Goodwife (1865-1901) was the sultan's third wife. She is the mother of Nâile Sultan.
- Mezîde Mestân (Mezîde Mestân) Third Goodwife (1869-1909), the fourth wife of the Sultan.
- Emsâlinûr Third Goodwife (1866-1950), other of Şâdiye Sultan.
- Ayşe Dest-i Zer Müşfika Fourth Goodwife (Müşfika Kayasoy-Kayıhan) (1872-1961), the mother of Ayşe Sultan. She was the most loved wife of the Sultan. She always accompanied the Sultan and remained his only wife after the dethronement. She was in Thessalonii with Sultan Abdulhamid and stayed with him in Beylerbeyi Palace until his demise.
- Favorites:
- Sâzkâr İkbal Leading Favorite (1873-1945 or 1950), the mother of Refia Sultan.
- Peyveste Second favorite (1873-1944), the mother of Prince Abdürrahim Effendi.
- Fatma Pesend Third Favorite (1876-1925), the mother of Hatice Sultan.
- Behîce (Maan) Fourth Favorite (1882-1969), the mother of twins Ahmed Nureddin and Mehmed Bedreddin Effendi.
- Sâliha Nâciye Fourth Favorite (1887-1924), the mother of Prince Âbid Effendi and Sâmiye Sultan.
- Mistresses:
- Dürdâne Hanım (1867-1955),
- Câlibos Hanım (1890- ?),
- Nazlıyâr Hanım

Offspring: Ulviye Sultan (1868-1875), Mehmed Selim Effendi (Mehmed Selim Osmanoğlu) (1870-1937), Zekiye Sultan (1872-1950), Nâime Sultan (Fatma Nâime Sultan) (1876-1945), Mehmed Abdulkadir Effendi and offspring (1878-1945), Ahmed Nuri Effendi (1878-1944), Nâile Sultan (1884-1957), Mehmed Burhâneddîn Effendi (1885-1949), Seniyye Sultan (1884-1884), Senîha Sultan (1885-1885), Şâdiye Sultan (Şâdiye Osmanoğlu) (1886-1977), Hamîde Ayşe Sultan (Ayşe Osmanoğlu) (1887-1977), Refia Sultan (1891-1938), Abdürrahim Hayri Effendi (1894-1952), Hatîce Sultan (1897-1898), Ahmed Nureddin (1901-1945) Effendi, Mehmed Bedreddin Effendi (1901-1903), Aliyye Sultan, Cemile Sultan, Sâmiye Sultan (1908-1909).

THE SULTAN'S IMPROVEMENTS AND PROJECTS

Instead of a one-way development of the state, Abdulhamid Han II commissioned the preparation of improvements and projects for the needs of the state administration and the nation in every field. Most of them were realized while others remained on paper as a project to be developed later. At the time, 72 million 780 thousand 129 gold coins were spent in over 1500 service establishments in each field. These include a number of state service buildings, mosques, hospitals, schools, workplaces, care and treatment facilities, roads, water, fountains and stations.

Just the titles of the projects commissioned by Sultan Abdulhamid Han's projects are as follows: Government Mansions, Municipal Offices, School Buildings, Hospital Buildings, Military Barracks Buildings, Patrol Buildings, Clock Towers, Transportation (Land-Sea-Port-Rail) Lines, Communication (Telegraph Buildings, Immigrant Neighborhoods, Irrigation Canals, Swampland improvement works, Bridge Construction, Horse Farm Facilities, Agricultural Facilities (GAP, Konya Plain), Petroleum Exploration-Facilities, Mine Exploration-Facilities, Photography of Historical, Natural and Governmental Works City Plans and Maps Studies...

The innovations made in his time in the areas of agriculture, zoning and education was enough to fill volumes of books.

He commissioned the building of water channels all over Ottoman territory and fulfilled the water needs of the people. Lake Terkos was a channel that brought water up to Yıldız Palace.

The Bosphorus and the Dardanelles straits were fortified. He repaired many military facilities and built new ones. Steps were taken for the first time regarding an underwater project and construction. The navy was fortified with new superior cruisers and battleships from Europe.

The Benghazi telegraph line was extended up to Medina-i Munevvere and cable was laid between Istanbul and Constanta. He commissioned the drilling of oil wells around Mosul and Kirkuk.

The Hejaz Railway project, which reached thousands of kilometers and would unite the Ottoman geography in terms of military, political, economic, religious and social aspects, was completed to a major degree. He had a project designed for a bridge over the Bosphorus between Rumeli-Kandilli and Üsküdar-Salacak tube tunnel project, many such projects were left unfinished when he was dethroned.

Sultan Abdulhamid had laid the foundations of the Southeastern Anatolia Project (GAP). Work was commissioned for preparing projects for the development of this region.

Between the years 1870-1890, the construction of the Rumelia Railways was completed and the Istanbul road was connected to Paris, Vienna and Berlin. During the reign of Sultan Abdulhamid Han (according to the statistics of 1896) the length of the railways was 1983 km on the European side and 1947 kilometers on the Anatolian side.

The other railway line that had started to be built was the Istanbul-Basra railway which would connect Istanbul and Islam countries. It was noteworthy that the Hejaz Railway, prioritized by the Sultan, was being entirely built by Muslim engineers and the cost were countered by donations from Muslims all over the globe. The Hejaz Railway, starting from Damascus and extending to Medina and Mecca, reached 1464 kilometers.

EDUCATION SERVICES

During the reign of Abdulhamid Han, the Ottoman Empire mobilized. Modernization activities in the field of education were paralleled with other modernization works. The activities that started with the Reform period accelerated during the reign of Abdulhamid Han. The educational institutions in provincial cities in particular became widespread and effective.

Officers were sent to Germany and other foreign countries for training for the modernization of the army.

Importance was given to vocational and technical education during this period. Trade and vocational schools were opened. Importance was given to the teaching of foreign languages in the high schools in port and trade cities to educate future traders.

During the reign of Sultan Abdulhamid, it was manifested that religious studies and sciences could be explained together in modern schools and major steps were taken in the area of national education. The number of junior high schools in 1876 when he succeeded the throne was 250 and reached 900 in 1909, and most of them delivered learning in their own buildings which had been built for this purpose.

The number of junior high schools was increasing and their qualities were being raised, but ultimately they corresponded to primary school and secondary schools. This time high schools were opened to give deliver corresponding education. The number of high schools which was 6 reached 109, and the number of students was 20 thousand. In 1877, there were only 200 modern elementary schools in Istanbul, and in 1905 this number reached 9,000. An average of 400 primary schools were opened each year.

Schools opened by Sultan Abdulhamid:

Law school (Mekteb-i Hukuk-ı Şâhâne), science, literature, medicide (Mekteb-i Tıbbiye-i Mülkiye-i Şâhâne) and political science (Mekteb-i Mülkiye-i Şâhâne) faculties,

Technical University (Mekteb-i Şâhâne-i Hendese-i Mülkiye)

Marine Engineering School (basis of current Naval War Academy)

Mekteb-i Harbiyeler (basis of current War Academies)

Military Veterinary School

Halkalı High Agronomy and Veterinary School

Sanayi-i Nefise Mektebi (basis of the current Fine Arts Faculty)

Hamidiye Ticaret Mektebi (Foundation of Academy of Economics and Commercial Sciences)

Tribal School (giving the idea of Ottomanism to the children of Arab and Kurdish tribes)

Harir Darütta'limi and Harir Darüttahsili schools (Foundation of the Sericulture Institute)

Viticulture and Cooking School

Faculty of Forestry and Mining

Police and Application School

Shepherd School

Higher Teacher School

Higher School of Commerce (Current Academy of Economic and Commercial Sciences),

Language Schools

Various faculties and universities in Damascus, Baghdad, Beirut, Konya and Thessaloniki

Vocational schools for boys and girls

Schools for the Disabled (deaf-mute-blind)

A high school in almost all province centers and thousands of secondary schools in districts.

HEALTH SERVICES

Abdulhamid Han, who was working on modernizing and institutionalizing the health services of the Ottoman Empire, took care to train health personnel, especially doctors and pharmacists. He followed the discoveries and inventions abroad and tried to transfer these developments into the country in a short time. In addition to Istanbul hospitals, Anatolian hospitals, Rumelia hospitals, Middle Eastern hospitals, Saudi Arabia and North Africa hospitals, military hospitals, Gureba hospitals, Hilal-i Ahmer hospitals, Syphilis hospitals and veterinary hospitals he commissioned the establishment of Haseki Nisa Hospital for women, Hamidiye Etfal (Children's Hospital), Navy Hospital, Haydarpaşa Medical School to establish hospitals on three continents to deliver medical services for all the subjects of the Ottoman State.

In addition, in order to advance medicine in our country, he sent physicians to international medical and health congresses held in Vienna, Paris, Lyon, Copenhagen, Dresden, London, Brussels, Rome, Moscow, Venice and Naples and followed the measures and scientific decisions taken there, and commissioned the application he considered beneficial for the people.

INDUSTRIAL BREAKTHROUGHS

Sultan Abdulhamid Han, as in every field had made great strides in industry. Large, medium and small-scale enterprises were opened for the development of industry and trade. Great importance was given to the development of industry and trade, and the contributors were honored by the sultan with gold and silver merit medals.

On the one hand, industrial and agricultural schools were opened and qualified personnel were trained for production, while factories and workshops were opened to expand domestic production.

New shipyards and shipbuilders were opened.

Carpet, fabric and yarn factories were among the main established factories. Each of these factories has its own history. It will suffice to write their names here:

Rolled down in the ceremonial room in Shale Pavilion, this very carpet was personally designed by the Sultan himself.

Bandırma Carpet Factory, East Carpet Company, Hereke Fabric and Carpet Factory, Karacabey Carpet Production House, Carpet Factory in Anatolia, Syrian Humus Carpet Factory, Eyup Defterdar Fes and Wool Fabric Factory, Fes and Melbusat-ı Military Factory, Darülaceze Hamidiye Fes Factory, Bakirkoy Cloth Factory, Bursa Silk and Weaving Factories, Izmit (Kocaeli) Cotton Fabric and Cotton Yarn (Çulhane Factory) Factory, Edirne-Cotton Fabric and Cotton Yarn Factory, Iraq-Mosul Weaving Industry, Aleppo Fabric and Cotton Yarn Factory, Thessaloniki Fabric and Cotton Yarn Factory, İzmir Silk-Cotton and Fabric Factory, Adana Military Outfit Factory and Dye Workshop, Rize Linen Cloth Factory, Beirut Silk Fabric Factories, Tripoli Silk Factories.

Paper, Tile and Glass Factories: Beykoz Paper Factory, Beirut Paper Factory, Tile, Porcelain and Glass Factories, Yıldız Tile and Porcelain Factory, Paşabahçe Glass Factory, Çubuklu Glass Factory.

Civilian Factories: Kucukcekmece Match Factory, Beirut Match Factory, Beykoz Shoe Factory, Diyarbakir Leather and Shoe Factory, Mosul Leather and Shoe Factory, Beirut Leather and Shoe Factory, Brick and Tile Factories, Iron Factories, Thessaloniki Cannery, Konya Potassium Nitrate Factory, Town Gas Station Centers, Diamond Processing Factory, Oil Plants, Flour and Ice Plants, Spermaceti Wax Factory, Pasta Plants

Military Factories: Seyandir Cannon Factory, Fuse Factory for Cannons, Tersane-i Amire Cannon Materials Factory, Mauser Rifle Spare Parts Factory, Ammunition Factories, Cartridge Factory, Gunpowder Factory, Ansaldo Factory,

Main Workshops: Various Weaving Looms, Clock Shop, Iron Machine Workshop, Photography Workshop, Paint Workshops, Soap Works, Sesame Oil Mill, Ginning Works, Lumber Works, Horseshoe Manufacturing

The Sultan laid railways to reach every corner of the country to extend production.

BRIDGE AND TUNNEL PROJECTS

Sultan Abdulhamid Han's continuation of the building activities included a bridge and a tube tunnel project to connect the Anatolian and Rumelian side. However, these projects would remain unfulfilled with the dethronement of the sultan.

Two bridges on the Bosphorus: During the reign of Abdulhamid II, the project was designed to connect the Bosphorus with two bridges, namely Sarayburnu-Uskudar and Rumeli Fortress-Kandilli.

The project was drawn by French civil engineer F. Arnodin in 1900. The aim of the project was to transport wagons from the bottom of the transfer bridge between Sarayburnu and Üsküdar by cable cars.

The planned bridge between Rumeli Fortress and Kandilli was called "Cisr-i Hamîdî" (Hamîdiye Bridge). The plan was to pass the railway from outside the city with the stations to be established in Bakırköy and Bostancı.

The bridge would be connected to the Bağdad railway line and it would be possible to disembark in Vienna when the Medina-i Münevvere train was boarded.

The Hamidiye Bridge was to be decorated with minarets and domes on two large pillars. The bridge would also be useful for military defense with cannon and rotating towers on the bridge, keeping the strait passage under control. The bridge included dedicated roads for trains, cars and pedestrians.

Submerged tubular tunnel projects: Work was also carried out in order to provide transportation from the sea in Ottoman Istanbul. Numerous projects were drawn for the construction of a tube passage.

The first submerged tube project was prepared by Eùqène Henri Gavand and presented the Ottoman government in 1876 with a tube passage project between Boğaziçi, Sarayburnu and Üsküdar.

The other project that connects Sarayburnu - Üsküdar (Şemsipaşa - Salacak) with the tube passage was prepared by the French S. Preault Railway Company.

In 1891, the 'Submarine Steel Tunnel' was presented by French Railway Engineer S. Preault. This underwater tube passage was going to be for railway transport.

Another tube passage project was planned on the Bosphorus (Üsküdar-Salacak) and Rumelia (Yenikapı-Sarayburnu) side. A new project was designed by Americans Frederic E. Strom, Frank T. Lindman and John A. Hilliker. The project was designed in 1902 and the bridges were designed with steel technology.

This tube passage called "Tünel-i Bahrî" was passed over 16 large columns fixed to the sea bottom. The tube passageway would operate two passenger and one freight carrying trains. The Harem section between Yenikapı and Harem would be connected to Haydarpaşa with a railway and continuous rail transportation between Europe and Asia would be ensured.

The tube passage projects, which were a continuation of the reconstruction activities carried out by Abdulhamid Han, were interrupted by his dethronement.

OIL EXPLORATION

In the Ottoman period, when the world industry and trade were dominated by the colonialists, one of the rivals of the British on Ottoman territory were the Germans. First the British and then the Germans asked for permission from Abdulhamid Han to carry out archaeological excavations on Ottoman territory. However, they were looking for oil. Britain, France and Germany had mobilized their political, military and economic powers in Mosul, Baghdad, and the region in order to take the region from the Ottoman Empire or acquire oil concessions.

Sultan Abdulhamid II conducted various surveys on the land and the oil-gas-mining exploration concession on the land was included in the treasury of the sultan, Hazîne-i Hâssa. Thus, these lands were protected from being bought by foreigners and from being lost in the event of any occupation.

French engineer Jakraz, who started to serve as a chief engineer in the Hazîne-i Hâssa Nezâreti in 1895, first reported his studies on the oil reserves around Baghdad and Mosul and presented them to the sultan with maps. German mining engineer Graskofp also carried out exploration work in the region and made a detailed oil map of the region.

However, the Union and Progress administration transferred the sultan's private property including from Hazîne-i Hâssa'e to the Treasury. Thus, the land with these precious metals would be invaded during the war period.

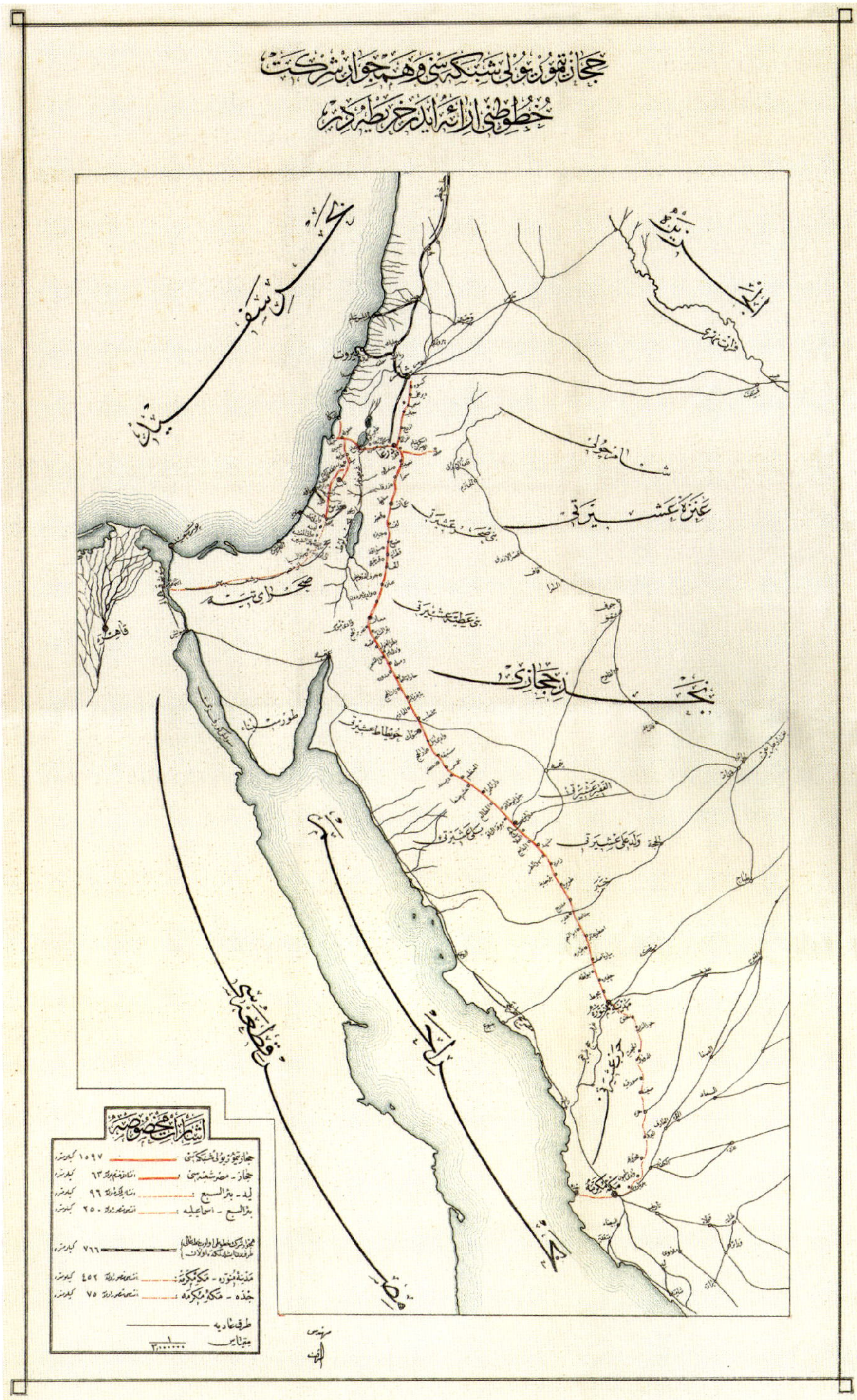

The map of the Hejaz Railway lines

Submerged tubular bridge designed and an American Engineer Fredrik E. Stro

Another submerged tubular bridge designed by a French Engineer named S. Preault

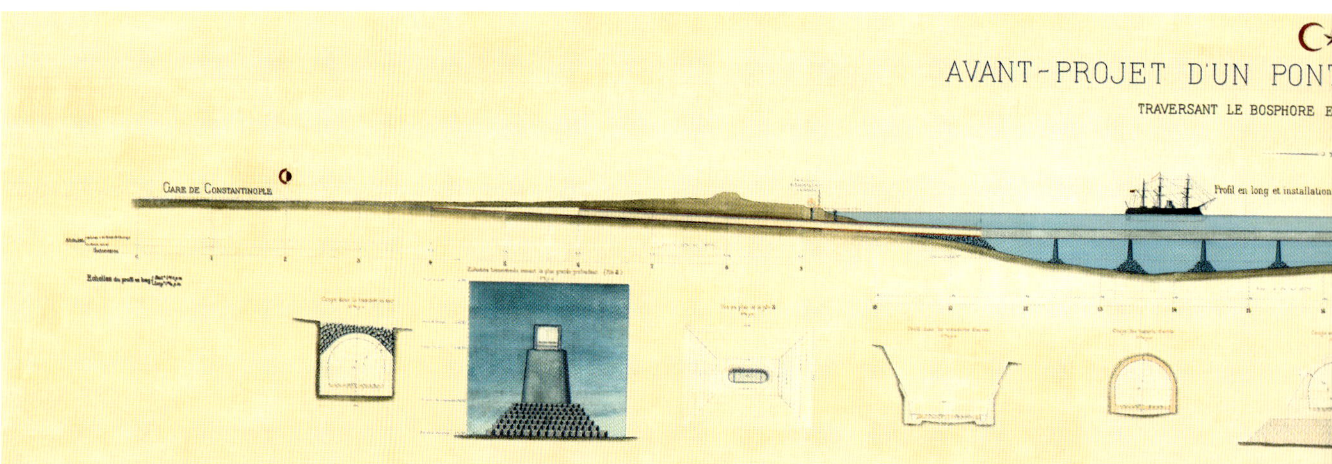

A bridge on Bosphorus envisioned by the International company of the Bosphorus railway

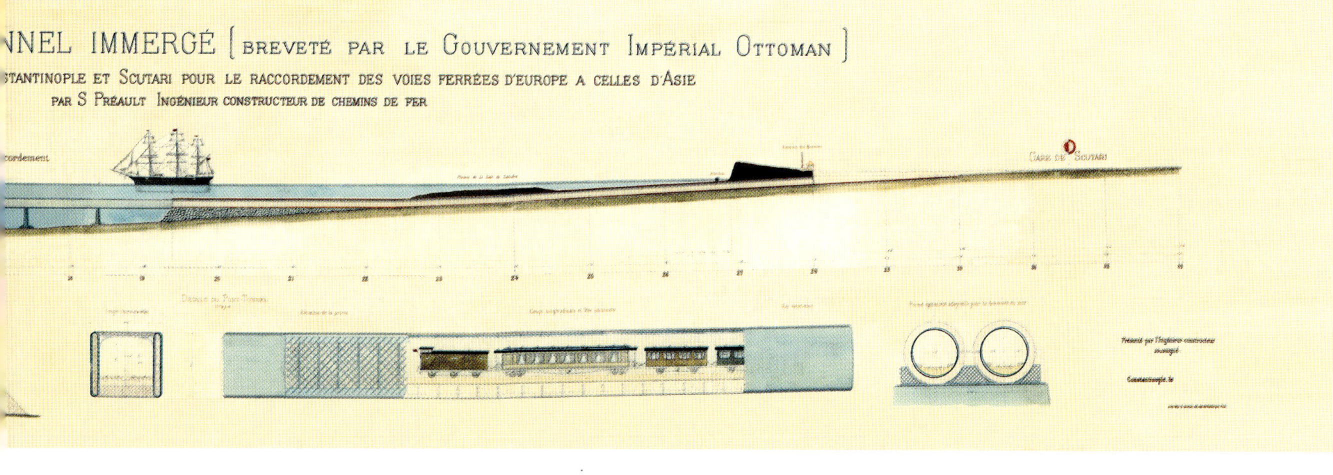

CHRONOLOGY OF THE SULTAN ABDULHAMID II ERA

21 September 1842: Birth of Abdulhamid II.

31 October 1852: His mother Goodwife Tirimüjgân passes away.

25 June 1861: His father Sultan Abdulmecid passes away.

1863: He travelled to Egypt with his uncle Sultan Abdulaziz.

21 June 1967: He travelled to European countries with his uncle Sultan Abdulaziz i.

1875

13 April 1875: Herzegovina rebellion.

25 April 1875: The Grand Vizier and Seraskier Hussein Avni Pasha were dismissed.

26 April 1875: Ministry of the Navy Sakızlı Es'ad Pasha's second viziership.

25/26 August 1875: The dismissal of Sakızlı Esad Pasha and the second viziership of Şûrây-I Devlet chief Mahmud Nedim Pasha the following day.

1876

2 May 1876: The Bulgarin rebellion called "April Revolution" in Bulgaria.

10 May 1876: The "Talebe-i Ulûm" (Mullahs) demonstrations organized by Midhat Pasha by distributing money lasted for three days.

11 May 1876: Mahmud Nedim Pasha was dismissed.

12 May 1876: Interpreter-Rüştü Pasha's fourth viziership and Hussein Avni Seraskiership, Midhat Pasha's ministry and Hasan Hayrullah Effendi's appointment to sheikdom united the "Erkân-i Erba'a" (the four men) in the same cabinet.

13 May 1876: Berlin memorandum.

30 May 1876: Sultan Abdulaziz's dethronement.

30 May 1876: Accession of Murad V, Prince Abdulhamid's promotion to crown prince.

4 June 1876: Sultan Aziz was martyred.

6 June 1876: Sultan Murad lost his mental health.

8 June 1876: Constitutional argument at Bâb-i Fetvâ (Fatwa Office).

15/16 June 1876: Hasan the Caucasian incident.

2 July 1876: War breaks out between Serbia and Montenegro.

31 August 1876: Murad V is removed from the Ottoman throne which he occupied for 93 days.

31 August 1876: Sultan Abdulhamid II succeeds to the Ottoman throne as the 34th sultan.

7 September 1876: Sultan Abdulhamid's Sword girding Ceremony.

31 October 1876: Russia's ultimatum regarding the suspension of the Serbia and Montenegro operation.

19 December 1876: Midhat Pasha's second viziership with the resignation of Interpretor-Rushdi Pasha.

23 December 1876: Shipyard Conference.

23 December 1876: Declaration of the I. Constitutional Monarchy.

1876: Loan crew payments were halted, the boarding schools in Izmir and Manastır (Bitola) were opened.

1877

18 January 1877: A 'general assembly' was held in Sublime Porte to examine and debate the proposals that were made at the shipyard conference.

5 February 1877: Midhat Pasha was dismissed and deported and Council of State head Edhem Pasha's viziership.

28 February 1877, Wedsnesday: The Serbian peace protocol was signed.

19 March 1877: Opening ceremony of the first Parliament.

24 April 1877: Russian Tsar declared war on the Ottoman State and the Turkish-Russian fight, called the 'war of 93', started.

4 June 1877: Britain Istanbul Treaty was prepared.

11 September 1877: Pleven victory.

10 December 1877: The fall of Pleven and Ghazi Osman Pasha falls prisoner.

Sultan Abdulmajid, Sultan Andulhamid's father

Dolmabahçe Palace, Constantinople

1877: Mahrec-i Aklâm, Mekteb-i Mülkiye was included in school classes and repealed. Medical School was returned to Gulhane, School of Technical Drawing and Architecture was established.

1878

11 January 1878: İbrahim Edhem Pasha was dismissed and Minister for Interior Ahmed Hamdi Pasha viziership.

31 January 1878: Russia and Edirne ceasefire.

4 February 1878: Ahmed Hamdi Pasha's dismissal and Minister for Education Ahmed Wafik Pasha's first viziership with the title 'Prime Minister'.

13 February 1878: Recess of the First Parliament that involved the state in war.

3 March 1878: San Stefanos Treaty was signed.

18 April 1878: Ahmed Wafik Pasha's dismissal and Mehmed Sadık Pasha's viziership.

20 May 1878: : The Ali Suavi incident called "Çırağan Incident".

28 May 1878: Mehmed Sadık Pasha's dismissal and Council of Ministers Interpretor Rushdi Pasha's fifth and last viziership.

4 June 1878: Turkish-British alliance against Russia and the Cyprus covenant.

4 June 1878: Interpretor Rüshdi Pasha's dismissal and Minister for Foreign Affairs Mehmed Es'ad Safvet Pasha's viziership.

13 July 1878: Signing the Berlin treaty with the Russians.

4 December 1878: Safvet Pasha's dismissal and Ayandan Tunuslu-Haydüddin Pasha's viziership.

1878: Serbia, Montenegro and Romania became independent separate countries. Bulgarian Princedom emerged, the Armenian issue manifested. Bosnia and Herzegovina was left to the occupation and administration of Austria-Hungary. The Macedonia issue emerged.

1879

29 July 1879: Hayruddin Pasha's (of Tunis) dismissal and Ahmed Ârifî Pasha's (of the notable) viziership with the title of 'Prime Minister'.

18 October 1879: Ahmed Arifî Pasha's dismissal and Minister for Justice Küçük (Younger) Said Pasha's viziership with the title of 'Prime Minister'.

1879: The Judiciary and Court Organization Law was enacted, Schools Pre-school Department was established, the central educational organization was re-organized, Criminal Procedure Law was enacted.

1880

13 March 1880: A school for girls was opened in Istanbul.

18 May 1880: One of the most important personalities of Reform literature Abdulhamid Ziya Pasha passed away.

20 December 1880: Darü'l-Fünun-ı Sultanî Law School has the first graduation.

9 June 1880: Said Pasha was dismissed and Mehmed Kadri Pasha's viziership with the title of 'Prime Minister'.

12 September 1880: Kadri Pasha's dismissal and Said Pasha's second viziership.

1880: Tax reform was made, Jaffa-Palestine railway line was completed. Rules of Procedure of the Civil Court were accepted; İstanbul Asâr-ı Atîka Museum (today known as Istanbul Archeological Museum) Glazed Tile Pavilion was opened to the public. An Agreement was signed between Turkey and Britain regarding the prohibition of trade in black slaves.

1881

12 May 1881: The principality of Tunisia was occupied by France.

2 July 1881: Tesalya and Narda provinces were left to Greece.

27 June 1881: the first session in Yıldız court in the interrogation of the murderers of Sultan Aziz.

20 December (28 Muharrem) 1881: "Muharrem Decree Law" and the establishment of National Debt.

1881: A new class was formed in the engineering school under the name of the distinguished class; The activities of Dârü bull-Fünûn-ı Sultânî Turuk u Maâbir Mektebi ended; Forest and Mining Schools were united.

1882

2 January 1882: Sanayi-i Nefise Mektebi (Fine Arts Academy) was established and Osman Hamdi Bey was appointed director.

2 May 1882: Said Pasha was dismissed and Abdurrahman Nurüddin Pasha of Kutahya became vizier.

10/11 July 1882: Abdurrahman Nurüddin Pasha resigned and therefore dismissed from the viziership.

11 July 1882: The British navy fired on Alexandria, occupied Egypt and Urabi Pasha resisted.

An album presented to the Sultan containing the images of some monasteries

12 July 1882: Said Pasha's third viziership under the title of 'Prime Minister'.

1 December 1882: Said Pasha's dismissal and Ahmed Wafik Pasha's second viziership.

3 December 1882: Ahmed Wafik Pasha's dismissal and Said Pasha's fourth viziership the following day.

1883

16 January 1883: Marmara University was established.

4 October 1883: the first European intercontinental express train, the Orient Express (Şark Ekspresi) disembarked from Paris on its maiden voyage.

1883: The Ottoman army was being improved by Prussian troops, Jamaleddin Afghani and Muhammed Abduh established 'el-Urvetü'l-Vüskâ', a reformist Islamic magazine in Paris.

1884

6/7 May 1884: Midhat and Son-in-law Mahmud Jalalüddin Pasha were strangled to death in the dungeon of Taif.

28 June 1884: Hacı Ârif Bey, a great composer who initiated the 'neo-classic' era in Turkish music passed away.

1 November 1884: The Civil Engineering School started its education in a room of Mühendishane-i Berrî-i Hümayun; the Fine Arts Academy was establish with the name Sanayi-i Nefise School.

1885

18 September 1885: Control in Eastern Rumelia province weakened when the governorate was granted to the Prince of Bulgaria and Eastern Rumelia united with Bulgaria.

24/25 September 1885: Said Pasha's dismissal and Minister for Pious Organizations Kamil Pasha's (of Cyprus) first viziership.

1886

1886: Adana-Mersin railway line was completed.

1886: Establishment of Non-muslim schools affiliated with the Ministry for Education and Department for Foreigners.

1886-1887: Turning Teachers' College into a boarding facility, establishment of Asia Society in Italy.

1887

13 November 1887: Bloody Sunday conflicts in central London.

1887: establishment of Yedikule Town gas factory, establishment of Hunchak society in Switzerland by Armenian nationalists.

1888

2 December 1888: Demise of Namık Kemal.

1888: Haydarpaşa-İzmir-Ankara railway concession was given to the Germans, veterinary class was included once again in War School.

1889

21 May 1889: İttihad-ı Osmanî Society (Union and Progress) was established in secret.

1889: a four year civil veterinary school based on schooling curriculum was established.

1890

20 June 1890: Armenian rebellion in Erzurum.

1890: Bulgarian, Macedonian and Armenian revolutionary gangs increased their activity, the Armenian demonstrations in Kumkapı in July.

1891

1 April 1891: The demise of Ahmed Wafik Pasha.

3/4 September 1891: The dismissal of Kamil Pasha and Kabaağaçlızade Ahmed Jevad Pasha's viziership.

3 November 1891: The opening of Teachers' College Âliye branch.

1891: Moving the Civil Veterinary School to the School of agriculture in Halkalı as a boarding facility, establishment of the Kadıköy - Kurbağalıdere Town Gas factory; opening the carpet section of Hereke Factory, the opening ceremony of the building that was built next to Çiniliköşk and is used currently as the Old Eastern Works Museum and starting the construction work of the current Archeology Museum opposite it, starting the publishing of Servetifünun journal in Istanbul.

1892

1892: Haydarpaşa-İzmit railway line was commissioned into operation, the porcelain workshops in Yıldız were established by Abdulhamid Han II, Lexicographer and orientalist Redhouse passed away.

1892-1893: Armenian rebellion in Merzifon, Kayseri, Yozgat.

1894

10 July 1894: The Great Istanbul earthquake.

1894: Halkalı Agronomy and Veterinary School produced their first veterinary graduates, İmmaculée Conseption or St. Marie school was established, Armenian incidents in Sason; Thessaloniki-Manastır railway line was completed.

1895

25 May 1895: The death of Ahmed Cevdet Pasha, the author of Tarih-i Cevdet and Kısas-ı Enbiya.

8 June 1895: Cevad Pasha's dismissal and Said Pasha's fifth viziership.

30 September 1895: First turmoil generated by Armenians in Istanbul.

30 September 1895: Dismissal of Vizier Said Pasha.

2 October 1895: Kamil Pasha's second viziership.

7 November 1895: Kamil Pasha's dismissal and Minister for Interior Halil Rif'at Pasha's viziership.

1895: Galata Pier construction was completed, a ruling for the appointment of Turkish teachers to non-muslim schools was issued, Manufacture of smokeless powder in Baruthâne-i Âmire; an Armenian rebellion attempt in Marash in November.

1896

1 June 1896: An Armenian rebellion in Van.

26 August 1896: The first turmoil generated by Armenians by attacing the Osmanlı Bank Istanbul branch that would be called the "Bank Incident".

1896: The construction of the Istanbul-Thessaloniki railway line was completed at the end of three years; the Cretan rebellion exacerbated, the Eskişehir-Konya railway line was completed.

A writing set holding the monogram of the Sultan

A vase made in the Royal Workshop

1897

4/5 April 1897: 1876-77 The death of Osman Pasha, who had earned the title of veteran and great fame and reputation by his courage and heroism during his defense of Pleven during the Turkish-Russian campaign.

18 April 1897: Greek forces invade Crete, Greek gangs attack Ottoman borders in Rumelia. Greece declares war and launches a campaign.

31 August 1897: The Naval Museum was established by Major Suleiman Nutki under the name of "Museum and Library Administration" in the building belonging to the Mine Detachment Command within the structure of Tersane-i Amire.

4 December 1897: Ottoman-Greek peace.

18 December 1897: The continuation of the Cretan issue; the withdrawal of the Ottoman forces by granting autonomy to the island, accepting the Greek prince Yorgi as governor.

30 December 1898: Opening of Gülhane Military Medical School.

1897: Theodore Herzl, the founder of Zionism, introduced the principles of the State of Israel.

1900

29 October 1900: As a result of Abdulhamid Han's attempt, the ban on Turkish language in Azerbaijani schools was abolished.

31 August 1900: Establishment of Darü'l-Fünun-ı Şahane

1900: The construction of the Hejaz Railway was incepted; Istanbul docks construction was completed.

1901

5 November 1901: French navy lands troops on Lesbos.

18 November 1901: Said Pasha's sixth viziership.

1901: The second edition of Lügat-ı Tıbbiye is issued, Vidinli Tevfik Pasha passes away, gang activity in Macedonia increases and leading states intervene, Theodore Herzl meets with Abdulhamid Han in May.

1902

21 September 1902: The first Macedonia revolution.

23 November 1902: Cum'a-ı Bâlâ uprising.

23 November 1902: Preparation of a special reform plan for Macedonia.

8 December 1902: The appointment of Hüseyin Hilmi Pasha as the "general inspector" to Macedonia with comprehensive authority.

1902: The Yemen uprisings start again, chukka and serge looms were added to the Hereke Factory.

1903

14 January 1903: With the dismissal of Said Pasha, Avlonyalı Mehmed Ferid Pasha was appointed vizier.

2 August 1903: The Great Revolution which lasted three months started in Macedonia.

31 August 1903: A medical school was established in Damascus.

6 November 1903: Lessons started at the medical school built in Istanbul-Haydarpaşa.

25 November 1903: Macedonia reforms.

1903: Schools were mandated to six years.

1904

18 June 1904: the author of Kamus-ı Türki and Lexicographer Şemseddin Sami passed away.

29 August 1904: Murad V passed away.

1904: Haydarpaşa Dock was completed and opened for operation.

1905

21 July 1905: Armenians carried out an assassination attempt against Abdulhamid Han II.

26 November 1905: Lesbos was occupied by the states because of the matter of Macedonia's financial reform.

1905: Hereke Factory started manufacturing fez.

1906

1 October 1906: The Aqaba issue was handled and Caliphate politics stood up to British imperialism.

1906: The Hind Muslim Union was established.

1907

25 April 1907: Customs dues were increased.

1908

9-10 June 1908: Reval interview.

22 July 1908: Said Pasha was appointed vizier for the seventh time with the dismissal of Avlonyalı-Ferid Pasha.

23 July 1908: The declaration of the Second Constitutional Monarchy.

4 August 1908: Said Pasha's resignation and Kamil Pasha's third viziership.

3 October 1908: Abolishment of European control over Macedonia's reforms.

5 October 1908: The kingdom of Bulgaria, which declared the annexation and independence of Bosnia and Herzegovina to Austria, took the form of kingdom.

6 October 1908: Crete declared its joining Greece.

17 December 1908: The second Parliament was opened.

1908: Beykoz Leather Factory was affiliated with the War Ministry, the Ottoman Pharmacists Society was established, Ottoman Veterinary Association was opened, Ottoman Engineers and Architects Association was established.

1909

13/14 February 1909: Kamil Pasha resigned and Minister for Interior Hüseyin Hilmi Pasha was appointed vizier for the first time the following day.

1 April 1909: Albanian rebellion.

13 April 1909: "31 March Incident" and Minister for Foreign Affairs Tevfik Pasha's first viziership with the resignation of Hüseyin Hilmi Pasha.

14 April 1909: 'Adana incident' which is a bloody Armenian revolution.

19 April 1909: Operation Army reaches Yeşilköy. Starts entering Istanbul.

27 April 1909: 27 April 1909: Dethronement of Sultan Abdulhamid Han II, accession of Mehmed Reşad V. Abdulhamid Han is exiled in Thessaloniki.

9/10 June 1909: Editor in chief of "Sadây-ı-Millet" newspaper Ahmed Samim is murdered at the hands of the hitman hired by the Committee of Union and Progress.

3 July 1909: 'Churches Law' which caused the Balkan alliance.

1909: Non-muslims are subjected to conscription instead of a 'payment', Societies Law is enacted, Dental School is opened, a new school under the name of Forestry school is opened, Medical School is joined with Military Medical School and moved to Haydarpaşa, Muallimhane-i Nüvvab is called Medresetü'l-Kuzat, Civilian Engineering School is affiliated with the Ministry of Public Works and given the title Certified Engineer School.

A vase presented to the Sultan by the German Emperor Wilhelm II

1911

28 September 1911: The Italian ultimatum demanding the evacuation of Tripoli and Benghazi.

8 October 1911: The start of the Balkan war.

15 October 1911: Signature of Ottoman-Italian Peace and Ouchy covenants.

1 November 1911: Transfer of Sultan Abdulhamid from Salonika to Istanbul.

1913

23 January 1912: The Sublime Porte Raid and the Union and Progress Committee removing Kamil Pasha with bloody violence and replacing him with Mahmud Şevket Pasha as vizier.

21 July 1913: Retrieval of Edirne in the Second Balkan War and Balkan peace.

1913: Opening of the first girls' high school in Istanbul under the name of 'İstanbul Inas Sultanisi'

1914

14 May 1914: III. Parliament Term.

28 June 1914: The killing of Austria-Hungary crown prince in Sarajevo.

28 July 1914: Austria-Hungary declares war on Serbia.

1 August 1914: Germany declares war on Russia.

2 August 1914: Parliament is recessed indefinitely.

2 August 1914: Ottoman State and Germany sign an alliance treaty.

4 August 1914: Germany declares war on France, Britain declares war on Germany: the First World Starts.

10 August 1914: German war ships (Goeben and Breslau) are allowed to pass the Straits.

9 September 1914: Repeal of capitulations.

12 September 1914: A university with three branches is opened in Istanbul under the name İnas Darü'l-Fünunu

29 September 1914: Publication of Islah-i Medaris Regulation

29 October 1914: The Ottoman fleet opens cannon fire on Russian ports in the Black Sea.

11 November 1914: The Ottoman Empire, which has allied with the German and Austrian-Hungarian empires, declares war against the states of Britain, France and Russia and enters the First World War..

14 November 1914: "Jihad-i Ekber" (Holy War/WWI) is declared by Mehmed V.

14 November 1914: İnas Sanayi-i Nefise School is opened.

18 December 1914: Egypt is transformed into a 'kingdom' under the auspices of Britain, Ottoman State law is ended.

21 December 1914: Sarıkamış operation starts followed by the Sarıkamış disaster.

1915

24 April 1915: The Armenian committees that operated against the Ottoman State were closed. 235 administrators of these committees who were anarchists were arrested.

25 April 1915: The enemy landed troops in Çanakkale strait.

3 May 1915: Armenian massacre in Van.

27 May 1915: The Relocation Law was enacted and the Armenian population that cooperated with the Russians in Eastern Anatolia was settled in central areas.

19/20 December 1915: The enemy starts withdrawing from the Çanakkale front.

1916

11 March 1916: Baghdad fell.

1917

25 March 1917: Sharia courts were affiliated with the Ministry of Justice.

6 April 1917: United States of America joined the war and declared war on Germany.

9 December 1917: Palestine fell and was lost.

1918

10 February 1918: The demise of Abdulhamid II and his burial in the Sultan Mahmud II Tomb in Divanyolu.